BUILDING THE BUSINESS OF "U"

LEAD | COMMUNICATE | CONNECT

Building the Business of "U": Lead, Communicate, Connect

Benedict Entertainment

Book design by:
Arbor Services, Inc.
www.arborservices.co/

Printed in the United States of America

Building the Business of "U": Lead, Communicate, Connect
Brian Benedict

1. Title 2. Author 3. Self-Help

Library of Congress Control Number: 2017915492

ISBN-13: 978-1979032131

ISBN-10: 1979032130

BUILDING THE BUSINESS OF "U"

LEAD | COMMUNICATE | CONNECT

BRIAN BENEDICT

Benedict Entertainment

This book is dedicated to

Toni Benedict.

Contents

Introduction **1**

Chapter One: The Leader in U **3**

Leaders Set an Example 7
Leaders Learn from Experience 10
Leaders Help Others Succeed 12
Leaders See Different Perspectives 14
Leaders Look Past Seniority 17
Leaders Are VIPs 19
Flashpoint Review! 23

Chapter Two: Character **25**

Courage 26
Loyalty and Selflessness 28
Honor 31
Integrity 33
A Reality Check 36
Flashpoint Review! 39

Chapter Three: Communication **41**

Duty 43
. . . Is Important Off the Job 45
. . . Motivates U to Think Long Term 48
. . . Helps U Connect with Your Team 50
Flashpoint Review! 52
Respect 53
. . . Pays Out What U Put In 55
. . . Helps U Stay Positive 57
. . . Conveys Interest in Others 59

Flashpoint Review! 64
Honesty and Genuineness 64
. . . Opens U Up to Connecting 65
. . . Shows U Value Others 68
. . . Reminds **U** to Listen 70
Flashpoint Review! 74
Empathy 74
. . . Connects U with Your Audience 75
. . . Breaks Down Defensive Attitudes 79
. . . Speaks to Minds and Hearts 82
Flashpoint Review! 85

Chapter Four: Communicate to Connect 87
. . . Simply and Effectively 88
. . . By Helping Others Connect and Grow 91
. . . To Safeguard Your Organization's Future 94
Flashpoint Review! 97

About the Author 99

Introduction

Brian Benedict is a leader and believes each person can achieve a level of influence regardless of position or title. His experience has spanned across the globe while being stationed in Karlsruhe Germany and Fort Bragg North Carolina to name a few while in the US Army. He eventually made a tough decision after re-enlisting and left the service as a single parent, raising his two year old daughter. He took his experiences, sacrifices and personal relationships and learned from each one he encountered as he left as an E-5 Sergeant.

During a time of advancing technology he was fortunate to be hired with Cellular One during the boom of the cell phone era. Like the army he climbed the ladder of success and learned the importance of handling people. The power of influence became vital to his growth and the company's growth. Being on the front lines he quickly realized that the first person customers make contact with becomes the face of the company no matter the size. Whether its a phone conversation or a personal one on one. The character and integrity of the lowest level of employee effects the daily growth of every operation.

After getting the opportunity to become a firefighter in 1996 he used this time to also enhance his off duty music and sales careers. The firefighting duties brought all the values he'd learned through the years into practice and became the next level in his life advancement. Even with the fire service you are the first impression of the department regardless if you're the private or chief of the organization. Whenever you're giving a tour, confronting a patient or providing medical services at a football game the way you conduct yourself is a direct reflection on the city, department and firefighters across the country.

Since retiring, Brian has been promoted from Department Representative with Police and Firemens Insurance Association to Midwest Manager. For the last decade he's helped police, fire and family throughout eastern Indiana and the Dayton Ohio Region. He currently helps and hires police officers and firefighters learn how to help those who help others. His passion continues to grow with purpose as the world is changing.

Brian has put together the 10 traits to becoming a Very Influential Person from his experiences with heroes in all walks of life. Commonalities not found in everyone but characteristics that can be learned and built. Brian strongly believe that titles, rank and position have little to do with influence. It begins with you.

Learn the 10 traits to becoming a very influence person and you to can become a VIP in your profession.

Chapter One: The Leader in U

In corporations, small businesses, government, and police and fire departments around the country, the story is the same. Men and women are being raised to positions where leadership is vital, yet many are never taught the difference between managing and leading. That difference is vital to your future success.

What is the difference, you ask? Influence. When influence is lacking, leadership is impossible. Followers feel frustrated, overlooked, and underutilized. They act on these feelings in a thousand destructive ways, further complicating the leader's job. If that sounds familiar, it may be because the organization you are a part of is suffering a leadership crisis. Most likely, training in vital leadership skills is lacking. Over time, a communication gap has opened between those expected to lead and those who must follow. Productivity has ground to a halt. The future of the organization itself, and of those who seek to rise within it, is in jeopardy.

Yet despite the seemingly insurmountable difficulties that come with working under the stress and strain of such a situation, there is a solution. If losing a generation (or more) of leaders is what got your organization into its current crisis, then the solution should be staring managers in the face. By any means possible, somebody has to rise to the challenge of putting leaders—real leaders—back in place. After reading this book and applying its insights, you will be able to say with confidence that the person with the skills to make the vital difference is **U**.

You are **U**nique. The knowledge you bring to your job, combined with your natural talents and hard-earned skills, represents a precious commodity to your department, your business, your organization, and all whom that organization serves. Nobody can do what **U**, the Unique you, can do. When you see that bold letter **U** in this text, remember that wherever you are in life right now, only through building the business of **U** will you find success. Contrary to the opinions of naysayers, nobody can replace **U** in your chosen field. Once you learn the value of influence and begin growing it for yourself, nobody will be able to limit you in your pursuit of achievement. No one can stifle your growth if you make uniqueness your commodity and sell, sell, sell. Even though your ability to chart your own future career path depends on several factors, by keeping **U** in the forefront of your mind, you'll be able to overcome any and all obstacles, blazing a path that no one else could blaze but that many will want to follow.

So, are you pepped up now, ready to take on the world? Hold that thought a minute. Nobody ever scaled Everest without first practicing hiking up a few steep hills. However driven you are right now, taking the time to build your stamina is well worth the effort. Consider this book your training guide to stepping up from a walk to a run in three specific areas: Leadership, Communication, and Connecting. Before you set out on your epic journey, you'd do well to consider its advice. Please note that I don't say "my advice." I make no claims to guruship in these pages. What I do lay claim to is experience, specifically the experience of being a leader.

I've seen good leaders and I've seen bad. I've seen people raised to leadership positions before they were ready. I've seen some flounder and some thrive. By observation, I've come to believe that every person can achieve a level of influence regardless of position or title.

My personal career path has spanned the globe, taking me from Fort Bragg, North Carolina, to Karlsruhe, Germany, among other US Army postings. After making the tough decision to leave the service, I was fortunate enough to work for Cellular One during the boom of the cell phone era. Riding the wave of emerging technologies, I achieved new heights of success and learned the power of influence with that company. The values I learned in the army, as a businessperson, and from Mom and Dad formed a strong foundation for my career in the fire service. It was as a firefighter that I learned most of the critical lessons that allowed me to step up as a leader.

Over the course of twenty years, I worked under some exemplary chiefs and served shoulder to shoulder with several strong leaders who held official rank or title. On my off days, I used my own uniqueness to build a music career. Later, I successfully sidelined as an insurance salesman, blazing trails that led me to my post-firefighting career as Midwest manager with Police and Firemen's Insurance Association. It's been my privilege over the last decade to aid police and firefighters throughout eastern Indiana and the Dayton, Ohio, region, using my leadership skills to benefit hardworking individuals dealing with a fall on hard times.

As you can see, my path to success has not always been a straight one, but it's gotten me where I am today. Looking back, I can tell you that the first, most essential step I took was making the commitment to become a leader. That is why the focus of this opening chapter, as the title suggests, is building The Leader in **U**.

What is a leader? A leader is a person of influence, someone others want to follow. A leader is a connector, one who builds a network of powerful personal and professional connections. Leaders have the ability to influence others and create positive change, regardless of their rank, title, or position. In organizations like the army, police, or fire service, the ability to connect inside the organization is vital to advancing your career. However, making connections on the outside can be even more essential. A forward-thinking leader, one who is invested in personal growth, must learn to connect both inside and out.

In the sections that follow, we'll talk more about what defines a leader. We'll discuss how important it is to Set an Example, to Learn from Experience, and to Help Others Succeed. We'll learn how valuable it can be for a leader to See Different Perspectives and Look Past Seniority. Finally, we'll learn how it is that we can say that Leaders Are VIPs. In chapter two, we'll discuss five Character traits essential to any leader. Chapter three will relate five Communication traits of equal worth. Finally, in chapter four, we'll revisit several of our core concepts, providing tips on how to Communicate to Connect.

Leaders Set an Example

As the twin sons of an air force soldier, my brother Bruce and I grew up feeling that the military was in our blood. We were seventeen when we signed on the dotted line. After graduating from high school on a Friday, we left for the army the following Sunday. Looking back, I think it must've been rough for my folks, being left with a big, empty house. At the time, my own future was such a big mystery that I wasn't thinking about anybody else.

During my enlistment I met many great soldiers who turned into terrific friends. After being stationed at Fort Jackson, Fort Gordon, and Fort Bragg, I reenlisted and was assigned to a concern—a German military base occupied by both German and American soldiers—in Karlsruhe. In the course of my travels I learned a lot about how leaders should conduct themselves. Unfortunately, I also imitated some examples that were less than great.

When, at age twenty, I was promoted to sergeant, I modeled myself after superiors who exploited their rank and position to boss people around. It didn't take me long to realize that this was a bad idea. Getting soldiers to obey my orders was a lot easier if I first connected with those under my command. Granted, making those connections took time, but I found that if I listened to my soldiers' concerns, sympathized with their frustrations, and praised their triumphs, they would reciprocate by helping me and the team willingly instead of me having to bully them. If only I'd been able to follow better examples, I would have spared myself a lot of headaches.

Military service was a great experience, and I'm proud that I served my country. Learning about leadership was a fringe benefit, but one I had to learn through effort. Despite all the regimens and routines I was taught in basic training, most of what I actually absorbed came from keeping my eyes open. The power of influence was something I noticed early and often. While I've never been the kind of kid who would walk off a cliff because somebody said so—Mom raised me with more sense than that—I found that the person whose influence prevailed was the one who set an example, not necessarily the guy barking orders.

In his 2011 book *The 5 Levels of Leadership*, John C. Maxwell detailed a paradigm that explains why I found some of the leaders I encountered over my military career easy to follow . . . and some not so easy. My own hardheadedness aside, I sincerely believe that several of the tough guys whose bossiness made me balk were stuck in a stage Maxwell calls *positional leadership*. Their claim on others' obedience was assigned from above, rather than being based on the essence of leadership, influence. Lacking that essence, they never came to understand the importance of building a team that follows voluntarily, not under compulsion. Worse, because these leaders weren't taught or didn't learn how to connect, they never reaped the enormous benefits voluntary submission can bring. We'll talk more about these benefits later. Sadly, in addition to being islands to themselves, these positional leaders felt content that the state of their character had brought them a measure of responsibility. Like the proverbial blind man who though the elephant's tail was a rope, they never got the big picture and remained unaware that continued character growth enhances every opportunity.

For all these reasons, those leaders were poor examples. I don't hold grudges, I'm not going to name names, but I would like to offer a point of contrast. Skipping ahead in my personal story, I'm reminded of a battalion chief I served under in Richmond FD in Indiana—a man named Jim Fessler. As BC over B-shift and department pension secretary, Jim saw it as his job to make connections across the organization, leading and educating his fellow firefighters. He was an easy man to follow, never slow with a joke—he could slice you up with a funny story before you realized that you were the butt—but was always ready to work hard.

If a structure fire got called in at two in the morning, Jim would be the first man out loading hose. Of course, if anybody on shift saw him doing it, we'd stop him immediately and take over. We had too much respect for Jim to let him do our job. Jim's honesty and dependability were an inspiration to us all. We always knew he had our backs. Taking orders from Jim was effortless, automatic. Often, he didn't even need to give any. We'd ask ourselves, "What would Jim do?" and do it before he had to ask.

Even if Jim hadn't held an official position as battalion chief, we would have looked to him for direction. Why? Because Jim set an example. His influence was character based and consensus approved. What do **U** think? Would you rather take orders from a stuck, positional leader or an influencer like Jim?

Leaders Learn from Experience

The United States Army is structured to help recruits advance. A system of achievements and goals rewards hard work. If a private gives his all, he'll be valued. That value will be reflected in medals and award ribbons to wear on the Class A uniforms. A general with a chest full of ribbons encourages the lower ranks to go the extra mile.

I was given my first opportunity to lead after years of having orders barked at me, first by drill sergeants, and later by commissioned officers and NCOs. Thanks in part to that reward structure I mentioned, I felt motivated to excel, to achieve whatever the army asked of me. Wearing my new corporal insignia, I was put in charge of a squad—a group of five to seven soldiers—in the 327th Signal Battalion. On the day I took command, I stood proud, thinking I had made it. All I had to do was give orders and watch my guys execute.

The problem was, I'd made it this far mainly on grit, not because I'd mastered the necessary skills. I hadn't yet learned what I needed to know about character, to say nothing about my communicating and connecting skills. You can imagine what happened. Day one, I barked orders. Day two, day three? Same thing. A couple weeks in, my squad went from welcoming me with open arms to grumbling at my slightest command. I saw it on their faces. I wasn't their buddy anymore. Inexperience and following the wrong examples had made me a roadblock in the way of their dignity and self-respect.

One night I got a call from the sergeant at the Charge of Quarters desk. A soldier of mine was out front with a gun, threatening to shoot himself. He'd requested me; I don't why. I considered him a friend, but my promotion and the way I initially handled my responsibilities had strained our relationship. Chain of command is drilled into recruits' heads from day one, so maybe I was the nearest thing to what he wanted, a familiar face close enough in age and rank to understand what he was going through. Whatever the case, I jumped into the car and arrived at the barracks in minutes. As I pulled up, I could see my friend out front, waving a pistol around and pacing. He was clearly distraught, angry, and confused.

The tension was thick. Barking orders wasn't going to help me now. As I got out of the car, it dawned on me that if I said the wrong thing, my friend might turn his anger on me. *Zigging* when I should *zag* could mean the end for us both. In order to help him, I needed to connect emotionally. But how? I asked myself, "If I were in his place, what would I want?" For someone to listen, I realized. So, that's what I offered. I didn't give an order, didn't tell my friend to stop being an idiot and stand down. I offered to listen. I didn't give a time table, either. Whatever he needed to say, for however long it took him to say it, I'd be there.

My strategy worked. My friend talked; I listened. He'd just found out that his girlfriend was pregnant with twins. For reasons of her own, she wanted to leave him. Man! No wonder he was stressed. After he settled down a bit, we sat on the picnic table in front of the barracks and talked for hours. I was scared. So was he. To set the example he needed, I had to feel a little of what he felt and set an example of how to cope. That night turned out to be one I'd always remember. Connecting with my fellow soldier was a gift. It helped him get through a tough patch and taught me an invaluable lesson. After that night, I took a genuine interest in the lives of my men. I talked to them about their families, about the struggles they faced behind closed doors.

In times of war, having the respect of the people you're trying to lead can mean the difference between life and death. It's no different in the fire department or in any position where service to others exposes a team to danger. My experience with my brother-in-arms was a wake-up call. It brought home to me the importance of communication in leadership. It also proved to me that there is no substitute for experience. Experience is the best teacher. Still, its lessons aren't absorbed automatically. A leader must remember, reflect on, and resolve to put into practice what they have learned. Only by letting the experience mold your thinking can **U** be equipped to share your experience with others and wield the influence of its wisdom.

Leaders Help Others Succeed

When my time in the military was up, I felt something was missing from my life. I recognized that something when I saw a classified ad in the newspaper. I had never given thought to being a firefighter, but when I saw that ad, I thought it might be a good replacement for the camaraderie I'd had with my fellow soldiers. But I didn't test right away. In fact, I had to wait two full years before a spot opened up in my local department. And my first impression of the department, when my chance finally came, was less than positive.

I was attending a seminar in Cincinnati when the chief called. So much time had elapsed since I'd submitted my application that his call came as a surprise. Still, I was glad the opportunity was open. Then I got a shock. According to the chief, if I wanted to move forward in the hiring process, I'd have to report for a physical the next day in Indianapolis. This seemed totally unreasonable. Two years after I submitted an application, this guy expected me to drop everything at a moment's notice? I told him I couldn't jeopardize my current job to try out for a position I might not get. He advised me that if I let my chance slip by, the department would move on to the next person in line. I said that was fine and consoled myself by concentrating on my career at Cellular One.

My job at Cellular One wasn't a bad gig, and I was learning. Developing interpersonal relationships, dealing with irate customers, and going for a win-win in every situation were training topics that have continued to benefit me to this day. The telecom world is, after all, a world of connections. I learned much about communication from working in the field. Military camaraderie was hard to give up, though, so when I got another invitation to test for the fire service, I jumped at the chance. Some months later, I began my firefighter training, and the rest is history.

Though my experience with the chief concerned me, I came to regard his actions as a good primer for the way some leaders operate. In the fire service, as in the military, some in high positions have the mindset that they don't have to accommodate anybody in the lower ranks. In the chief's mind, making a scheduling concession for a raw recruit wasn't worth his time. Later in my career, I learned that hardly anyone turns down the fire department when they get a call to test. As the chief told me, those who do are scratched off and forgotten. In fact, one of the traditional practices for pruning the hedges at most police and fire departments is to throw away any application that is missing information without regard to the quality of the applicant. I sometimes wonder how many young men and women who could have made "Firefighter of the Year" have been skipped over due to an error in paperwork.

I didn't bear the chief any ill will at the time, and I don't now. He had a list of folks to get through, and he didn't know me from Adam. However, if he'd taken more interest in my advancement, we both could have made a valuable connection. The positive impression this would have made on me may never have fed back to the chief in person, but I would have been able to give my all to the department at an earlier opportunity. The fact that I was extended a second invitation to test proves the department had a need at the time. How much extra work could have been spared if the chief had been just a little more flexible?

Helping other people reach their goals is one of the most powerful ways a leader can make connections with those who follow. It sets a sterling example and motivates everybody involved to work for the good of the organization.

Leaders See Different Perspectives

Before I was cleared to begin training as a firefighter, I was asked to submit to a polygraph at the local police station. *No sweat*, I thought.

At twenty-eight years old, with five years of military service and a clean record, I was sure this was a mere formality. I figured everybody involved would take the same attitude. Boy was I wrong!

On Friday evening, I arrived at the local PD. The detective who came to fetch me had a permanent scowl etched on his face. He led the way through the detective division to an interrogation room, never uttering a word. The police department was empty, I remember. We seemed to be the only people in the building, aside from a dispatcher at the front desk. The detective sat me down, strapped me in, and started asking questions.

By the time he was finished, I felt like I was about to go to jail as a drug addict, an alcoholic, a thief, and a murderer. I was happy my interrogator never broke out the handcuffs or ordered a strip search! So far as I could tell, he thought I was the scum of the earth. He liked me about as much as a pimple on the keister. I remember sitting in my car outside the police department wondering what I had done to make that guy so angry. This was another wasted opportunity to give me a good start on my new career.

Now, obviously, this police detective's bad attitude wasn't the fire department's fault. Thankfully, I was mature enough to realize that, so despite the bad taste in my mouth, I moved forward with testing and training. I felt like my purpose in life, the work that was going to make me happy, involved helping others. As a firefighter, I could serve the community, serve my brother firefighters, and utilize the leadership skills I'd learned in the army. Those goals were appealing enough that I got over feeling like crud on the detective's shoe.

Not until years later, after I became a fire investigator, did I come to a fuller understanding of the situation. The difference between real detectives and TV detectives is that real detectives have a life outside of work. Unless they're called out to a scene, they typically work a day shift, from seven in the morning to three in the afternoon. It was hours later than that when I showed up for my lie detector test. No wonder the detective was cranky! After years of battling interdepartmental politics and generational criminals, being exposed to a constant stream of individuals who couldn't tell the truth to save their mother's sainted lives, I could have been a Swedish bikini model and he would have given me the stink eye for making him work late on a Friday night.

Understanding his point of view would've made all the difference in our interaction. Instead of trooping out with a hangdog look, I could have used my exposure to this guy at his worst to get insight into the challenges he was dealing with. I could have made a connection! This time, the fault was mine. In the years to follow, I worked hand in hand with many different detectives, several of whom became lifelong friends. They taught me all about what it was like to lift their loads. My own work benefited as a result. If I had known what to look for way back when, I'm sure the detective who gave me the polygraph would have been a good guy to know.

As it happened, he retired before I got the chance to tell him about the lasting impression he'd made. Though that impression was negative at first, shifting my perspective taught me that you never truly know why somebody acts the way they do. Nobody is their own bad attitude, and bad attitudes don't come out of the blue. Accepting that the negativity people sometimes throw your way often has nothing to do with you is the first step toward progressing in a spirit of genuine understanding. Seeing situations from somebody else's perspective can help **U** connect, as well as spare you from hard feelings and regret.

Leaders Look Past Seniority

Though all the leadership deficiencies I've highlighted so far are, I believe, universal to organizations large and small, the problem I hear bemoaned often is the failure of positional leaders to spot talent in new recruits. I've seen this myself, I've been a victim of it myself, and I can readily identify one root cause. Positional leaders are blinded by seniority. Often, seniority is the only measure of a subordinate's worth such leaders know how to read. This isn't hard to understand. Positional leaders quite often make career advancements only by means of their own seniority. After all, if they had a better understanding of how to lead, they'd gain influence and get unstuck from that lowest leadership level.

After I left the army, I spent some months wondering what my future would hold. One evening, while pondering my future in a Richmond, Indiana, bar named Smiley's, a friend of mine told me about his new job installing car phones in vehicles. Like me, he had recently left the military. Like me, his prospects were wide open but a little daunting. As I considered following my buddy's example, my first thought was that having recently been responsible for soldiers, equipment, and important missions, car phone installation was a big step down. But I swallowed my pride and interviewed for the position, reasoning that no matter where I eventually found a job, it would more than likely be at the bottom of achievement hill. I'd have to prove myself to new people in a new environment. My military credentials, though meaningful to me, wouldn't register with a civilian boss. Again.

As it happened, the interviewer for the installer position had military experience himself. He was positive and encouraging. Soon, I began my new career. The starting pay rate was minimal, but thanks to the connections I made, I rose quickly through the ranks at Cellular One. Thinking about it now, it's remarkable the way my military connections helped me get into the job. I had felt demoralized, convinced that the skills I'd honed in the military would be discounted in the "real world." Yet thanks to my connections, I found that I had nothing to worry about. Plenty of people had walked in my shoes. Many were eager to extend a helping hand to a fellow veteran. My connections were a lifeline to these folks.

The concern I had that my military skills wouldn't be appreciated by anybody outside the military gets to the heart of the issue I have with seniority. Everybody brings special skills to a job, skills they learned from their previous employment, hobbies, and education. It behooves a leader to learn to recognize those skills and decide how they can be used to benefit the organization. Failing to do so can and does result in missed opportunities.

For instance, early in my firefighting career, I asked to represent the department at a meeting of the Chamber of Commerce. Even though none of my superiors intended to attend, the individual I asked looked at me like I was out of my mind. A wet-nosed kid making such a suggestion was unthinkable! It didn't help that the kid in question was a thirty-year-old family man with considerable achievements under his belt. Apparently my representation at the meeting was less desirable than no representation at all.

The negative response I received had nothing to do with my personal worth and everything to do with my lack of departmental seniority. My superior in that situation was blind to the qualities I could bring to the job of spokesman, despite that I'd been tested and proven my merit over a decade of military and business life.

As you grow yourself as a leader, don't make the mistake of overlooking each person's talents. Open your eyes to the potential of those you lead. Search for ways to help them meet that potential. This will help you connect with them on a personal level. Your influence will flourish as they achieve.

Leaders Are VIPs

Leading by example is a powerful influencer. Even when you're not on the job, the way you conduct yourself can positively or negatively impact the community. That goes double for a leader, since every person under you is going to be, at least at the start, a reflection of the example you've set. Individual examples, taken together, create the community's impression of the organization to which those individuals belong. Whether you're a new recruit, a rising star, or an expert in your subject, **U** have the power to influence what people think and how they behave.

Sometimes, we're our own worst enemies. We react without thought, make rash decisions, thump our chests, and tell an inquisitive subordinate, "Because I said so." Take a moment to think about some of your own interactions inside and outside your organization. Have **U** used your influence to build trust or to tear it down? We all have good days and bad, but what's the overall trend? To build others up we must first build ourselves. Those who become adept at this, and who use what they've built to lead others, are **VIPs—Very Influential People**. All of the positive examples I have and will mention are VIPs. To help you progress as a leader, growing the influence you need to step up into your own VIP role, I have broken down the topics the remainder of this book will discuss into **Ten Essential Traits of a VIP**.

In boiling down the qualities I'm about to recommend, I called upon experiences I've had in several different walks of life. Since the fire service has been such an important part of my personal development, I felt it appropriate to dig deep into what it means to be a dedicated lifesaver. You'll find that many of the examples I've selected are drawn from my time working with various fire and police departments. But make no mistake: A careful reading of these illustrations will demonstrate that the traits are important to every endeavor where leadership has value. They are traits we would all like to see in our supervisors and in colleagues exerting themselves to take the next positive step in their careers. Most importantly, they are traits that every VIP must cultivate within him or herself. By building these Essential Traits, you can grow in competence and personal preparedness, learn to increase and wield influence effectively, and inspire others to imitate your positive example.

The 10 Essential Traits of a VIP

1. ***Courage*—Facing your fears with calm and confidence**
2. ***Loyalty*—Being devoted to your team and department**
3. ***Selflessness*—Valuing the life and property of others more than your own**
4. ***Honor*—Living up to the highest standard of conduct**
5. ***Integrity*—Doing what is ethically and morally right**

***

6. ***Duty*—Feeling driven to fulfill your obligations**
7. ***Respect*—Treating others the way you'd want to be treated**
8. ***Honesty*—Always being honest and truthful**
9. ***Genuineness*—Being genuine and accountable in your actions**
10. ***Empathy*—Showing interest in understanding others**

As mentioned in the introductory section, this book will treat these traits as two lists. We'll discuss the first five in chapter two: Character. The remaining five will give structure to chapter three: Communication. As you read through these sections, consider how each trait relates to your personal circumstance. What bearing does it have on the example you set for others? How will improving in that trait help your influence grow? How will it benefit your organization?

Some people will read the descriptions of the Ten Essential Traits and laugh. A desire to advance in these traits wasn't why they got into their present career. Not everybody is going to recognize a direct line between courage, loyalty, selflessness, honor, integrity, duty, respect, honesty, genuineness, empathy, and leadership. If you have trouble seeing the relationship between leadership, influence, and **U**, consider what will happen if you don't step up to cultivate these traits. Organizations, like nature, abhor a vacuum. If you don't step up as a leader in your field, somebody else will. If you were tasked with choosing that person—somebody other than yourself to set the example your workmates will follow—what traits would attract you?

I'm reminded of a cleaning lady I used to know. She was a professional house cleaner for years while serving in a position on the city council. While still holding down her day job, she decided to run for mayor. She figured the connections she'd made gave her as good a shot as anybody. And she was right. She became one of our city's rare three-term mayors. Her honesty, respect, genuineness, and empathy for people out there struggling made it easy for people to pledge their support to this outstanding public servant. Those traits made her a VIP. Despite not being born to wealth or spending years earning a degree, the mayor was able to connect with voters, as well as fellow leaders. Because she cared about people, she put work into leading. Her success speaks for itself.

It's okay to have doubts. Having doubts and still taking action is the essence of courage. Don't let doubts hold you back. If you are lacking in any of the Essential Traits, take the initiative to ensure you can meet the demands of an assigned position. Remember, positional leadership is the ladder's lowest rung. Plenty of great leaders don't start out appointed to a position. They start out building relationships, connecting with people who then choose to let them lead. John C. Maxwell calls this *permission leadership*. It's the followers who give permission, says Maxwell, not those above. The situation is democratic and merit based. Don't we all want leaders we can feel good about following?

Let's make this personal. Leadership is about what **U** do when opportunities come your way. Sometimes those opportunities come from above, in the form of a new position. Sometimes they come about because folks at your same level are looking for somebody to follow. No matter where they come from, your response to opportunity is what makes the difference. So what about you? Will you take what you can get for as long as you can fake it? Or will you build on the essential traits and become the best leader **U** can be?

Flashpoint Review!

For readers unfamiliar with the term, a flashpoint is the temperature at which a given substance ignites. We'll use these concluding sections to touch on main points, in the hope of keeping your brain cells fired up.

- Leadership is influence.
- You don't need rank or position to be a leader.
- New recruits look to leaders as examples, so it's important to be a good one.

- Helping other people is a great way to connect.
- Nobody is their bad attitude.
- Everybody, even raw recruits, brings something valuable to the job.
- By building 10 Essential Traits, you can be a **Very Influential Person**.

Chapter Two: Character

A leader must be of excellent character. Why? Because leaders have to be strong. If you were inspecting masonry after a structure fire and found severe cracks, would you advise the homeowner to place additional load on the affected bricks? Of course not. Similarly, if a leader demonstrates selfish tendencies, is prone to being dishonest, or has a hard time treating others with respect, those qualities won't improve when the leader is under fire, so to speak. Usually, such cracks—deficiencies in character—become more obvious. On the other hand, character can be forged under pressure. It takes thousands of years for a lump of coal to harden into a diamond. That hardening happens with the weight of the world pressing down. VIPs are no different.

Picture an exemplary firefighter handling questions from a member of the community at the scene. This is a guy who's either just been inside a burning building or has orchestrated the attack from the outside, with lives on the line. Attacking a fire requires full engagement of the will and senses. Firefighters have to put fear, self-interest, and personal doubt aside, sometimes for hours at a time. No matter how difficult the task, they have to keep moving forward. Once a firefighter has turned that kind of focus on, it takes time to turn it off, biologically as well as emotionally. Yet, firefighter officers are often approached by civilians, people who will encounter only a few emergencies in their lifetime, while the smoke's still rising.

How do firefighters connect in situations like that? Only through strength of character. Likewise, a leader under fire needs courage to not give in to fear; loyalty and selflessness to work with others as a team; honor not to leave a job half done; and integrity to keep from passing the buck or inflating their own ego. All these traits are essential to decreasing stress and connecting with others facing similar challenges. A person who doesn't develop these traits will never be a VIP. One who works hard to excel at them will be a leader worth following.

Courage

Deputy Chief Pete McDaniel is a good friend of mine, long since retired from firefighting. He's a true one-of-a-kind. With him being a marine and me being army, we traded lots of jabs over the years. Still, we've always respected each other. One experience in particular made me realize what an example of **courage** he really is.

Our units were called to a fully involved single-story house fire on the northwest side of town. The crew was Pete with Lieutenant Oscar Abner on Rescue, Engineer VanMeter, Lieutenant "Rat" Rantanen, and me on Engine One. Hitting the ground running, I pulled an inch-and-three-quarter hose to the house while Pete tried to enter. He found the door blocked, with just enough space for a man to squeeze through. Now, a clear exit strategy is as important to a firefighter as it is a general, but Pete, Rat, and I weren't going to let an impediment get in the way of doing our job. We pushed in for the charge. All of us were experienced firefighters, but we had a job trying to maneuver around fallen ceiling material, furniture, and other obstacles impeding our progress.

As we fought our way through one smoke-black room, Pete and I crawled over a moped lying on its side. In zero visibility, Pete felt around and recognized a human body part. He alerted me and I handed Rat the line, while Pete and I tried to move the victim outside. The lifeless individual had adhered to the moped and the carpet. Despite our efforts, we were unable to detach him. I expended enough energy, on top of the effects of adrenaline, that I was overcome with exertion. I threw up in my mask and had to crawl outside to vent. Pete kept his cool and guided me back, then led the way deeper into the inferno, seeking its point of origin.

We had moved another ten feet when I heard Pete make a noise. He was snagged in wires snaking from the ceiling and was unable to move. It was touch and go, but Pete didn't panic. Finally, he was able to wrestle his way out. After a major team effort, the fire was extinguished. During the overhaul and investigation, we learned that the victim was a familiar face in the community, known for puttering that moped around town. Investigators believed that he tried to drive his vehicle out of the house before being overcome by smoke inhalation. It was a sad story, but the part we firefighters played could have gone a lot worse if I hadn't had a tough, courageous professional like Pete

McDaniel by my side. By staying focused and keeping his head in the game, Pete continued to be an asset to the team, even in difficult circumstances.

His performance that day was impressive, but not surprising. Pete is a guy who practices what he preaches. For the duration of his career, he did what it took to accomplish the mission. Faced with adversity, he persevered, inspiring his team to follow his example. The hallmark of a good leader is to be somebody people want to imitate. I was fortunate to get a chance to learn from Pete's courage as a firefighter. His leadership made a lasting impression on me.

Loyalty and Selflessness

"No man ever wins the loyalty of troops by preaching loyalty. It is given to him by them as he proves his possession of the other virtues."—Brigadier General S. L. A. Marshall, Men Against Fire *(1947)*

In harmony with what the general said, leaders earn **loyalty** by displaying honor and integrity, qualities we'll discuss later on. Leaders build trust by getting down in the trenches, and even more importantly, by protecting those who live there. A good leader never lets those under their charge be misused or abused. A VIP excels by standing by the team.

Loyalty and trust are tested when emergencies occur, but these qualities have to be built beforehand. To create strong bonds, the team has to know each other, and the leader has to know each member better than anybody else. Is somebody having family trouble? Are they sick? Are they mired in debt, with bill collectors knocking at the door? Loyalty is going to move a leader to help that teammate cope. In return, when the leader asks that teammate to pull her weight, the response will be positive and immediate. When things fall apart at home, the team should be a haven, a place of safety where the individual is appreciated, so that everyone can give their all.

The relationship between loyalty and **selflessness** is a feedback loop. Being selfless means putting others' needs ahead of your own. An individual who helps others through selfless service inspires loyalty. Loyalty inspires others to give selflessly. A team whose members are loyal to each other and selfless in doing their collective duty is an asset to any organization.

So, how can a leader inspire loyalty and move others to selfless service? Setting an example is key. The leader must be focused on helping others, communicating that attitude by genuinely caring about the team, their families, and the people the organization is called upon to serve. Anthropologist Robin Dunbar estimates that people feel genuinely comfortable only with the closest 150 people in their social circles. These are the people you wouldn't feel awkward joining for a drink at the bar if you met them by chance.[1] Beyond that tight-knit few, you're going to hesitate. How long probably depends on how thirsty you are, but the point is that we don't instantly feel buddy-buddy with every person we meet. It takes effort to develop

---

1 Robin Dunbar, *Grooming, Gossip, and the Evolution of Language* (Cambridge, MA: Harvard University Press, 1998), 77, ISBN 0674363361, Retrieved 17 December 2016.

genuine concern for others. You've got to dig deep, helping each other out on bad days, getting to know your team member's circles, even if they don't overlap with your own.

When it comes to giving selflessly to the community, find the common denominator in relationships that makes you feel comfortable. What do you like about your three best friends that makes it easy to hang out with them? Some common thread draws you all together and keeps you close, even when you're ragging on each other. Once you identify that thread, look for how others fit in. Do they have similar hobbies? Similar goals? What about their background can you relate to? In binding yourself to others in this way, you're not necessarily trying to find a new best bud, just to get a little appreciation for a person you may have to depend on when the going gets tough.

Abraham Lincoln said, "If you would win a man to your cause, first convince him that you are his sincere friend." Lincoln was a great leader and a gifted connector. He knew that helping others is more satisfying than achieving selfish goals. In my years as a representative for Police and Firemen's Insurance, my favorite part of the job has been helping the newly injured. When I get an alert about a police officer or firefighter who has recently been hurt, I give it my full attention. I routinely travel an hour or more to sit with guys at the hospital after an ACL or rotator cuff surgery. Sometimes, I visit them at home during recovery. I don't show up in person to give insurance advice. I could do that over the phone. I want people to feel comfortable and don't mind taking the time. Contacts I've made in this way have stuck with me for years, and family members have told me how important my visits were. It doesn't cost much, and I enjoy doing it. Selfless service is its own reward, but a leader knows that the loyalty it inspires creates connections that can last a lifetime.

Honor

Honor, for a firefighter, means conducting ourselves in a way that reflects well on the department and our profession as a whole. To quote the National Society of Executive Fire Officers, in their Firefighter Code of Ethics:

> Character is not necessarily defined by how a person behaves when conditions are optimal and life is good. It is easy to take the high road when the path is paved and obstacles are few or nonexistent. Character is also defined by decisions made under pressure, when no one is looking, when the road contains land mines, and the way is obscured.

Showing honorable, ethical character means that when we give our word, we follow through with consistent action. Accepting responsibility, even when it entails more work for ourselves, demonstrates to others that we are worthy of their trust. Since we have to trust each other with our lives, firefighters don't let minor disagreements drive a wedge between ourselves and our brothers. When in the public eye, we elevate our standards above what others expect of us. Not every profession values honor so highly. Being able to trust the word of my workmates wasn't a matter of life and death when I was in cell phone sales. But when it comes to building the business of **U**, being known as an honorable person can do amazing things for your personal brand.

Conducting yourself honorably often requires taking a step back, refusing to let circumstances prescribe your behavior. I personally remember fighting many fires where a family's life was changed. Some lost precious pictures and favorite heirlooms. Others, beloved pets or family members. When you're en route to a fire, you never know exactly what you're getting into. Dispatch can only report what they hear, and situations can change by the time first responders arrive at a scene. A firefighter who acts with honor must be prepared to take and carry out orders in circumstances where the right course of action doesn't seem clear cut.

Honor is also tested after a fire is brought under control. A firefighter performs challenging feats during a fire attack, making entry, crawling, breathing through a mask, and generally making order out of chaos. After the operation winds down, we often spend time putting out hot spots so the fire won't rekindle an hour later. During this period, news media and cell phone photographers tend to congregate, filling the sidewalk. Standing orders in most departments warn firefighters not to joke around after the danger has passed. Fighting a fire builds tension, and giving vent to that tension by firing off cynical jokes and zingers can create problems of perception in the public eye.

After a serious incident, keeping the community's perspective in mind can be tough for firefighters. Even if we're not boisterously jerking somebody's chain, our nonverbal communication can convey the wrong impression. Appearance and body language are what the camera sees, after all. That's why firefighters work to show a respectable demeanor even while adrenaline is pulsing through their veins. After firefighters leave the scene, of course, is another story. Blowing off steam behind closed doors is a time-tested tradition in fire departments. Honor makes clear to a firefighter the difference between easing tension and being an embarrassment to the service.

Even if you're not a professional lifesaver, no doubt the organization you belong to has a reputation to uphold. Perhaps they're even looking to improve that reputation. Such a situation creates an opportunity for you to increase your influence by showing honor. Holding the organization's reputation in the forefront of your mind will equip you to walk the line between doing your job and putting on a good face when in the public eye. This is no sham appearance of propriety. To behave honorably, you must govern your actions and reactions, not being concerned only with benefiting yourself, but your employers, colleagues, and friends. This requires more than simple professionalism. Professionalism motivates an executive to put on a tie before going to work. Honor will move that executive to think carefully about every interaction and give due attention to appearances even when nobody appears to be around to watch. In short, honor means acting on loyalty and selflessness, and the integrity that will be the topic of our next section.

Integrity

Closely related to honor is the concept of **integrity**. It's a synthesis, in many ways, of courage and honor. Having integrity requires being clear and consistent in your principles, having high moral standards, and esteeming honesty and truth. If an assigned task cannot be accomplished, a leader with integrity will inform somebody up the chain of command, rather than trying to hide the problem. A leader with integrity will never lie about the preparedness of an apparatus or equipment but look to address the deficiency with honor. A leader with integrity who accidentally passes on bad information will correct the mistake as soon as possible, setting aside fears that this will reflect badly on one's abilities.

Integrity gets a leader ready to accept responsibility for imperfect actions. We all make mistakes. Integrity builds trust that the mistakes aren't what define us. It inspires honest dealing, setting an example for others to follow. If the powers that be are smart, they won't appoint a deceitful leader. Lying is highly contagious. Imagine living in a community where the fire chief is known for lying. How confident would you be calling 9-1-1? When it comes to first responders, communities need to know that they're putting their lives into trustworthy, professional hands. A fire department that loses its reputation for integrity will quickly find itself at odds with community leaders. A businessperson without integrity can expect customers to express their concerns by closing their wallets. Integrity must be present in a successful organization from top to bottom and from bottom to top.

Courage factors into integrity when doing the right thing requires a leader to work against his or her own interests. America's top World War I fighter ace, Captain Eddie Rickenbacker, said, "Personal courage is not the absence of fear. It is the ability to put fear aside and do what is necessary. Personal courage takes two forms: physical and moral. Good leaders demonstrate both." By standing firm on values, principles, and convictions, a leader demonstrates courage in the service of honor, our recipe for integrity.

Even when things don't go their way, VIPs stand up for what they believe is right. Once, while preparing on-boarding paperwork for a new insurance representative, I checked a box that indicated the rep wanted to be paid his commission as earned, rather than upfront. This meant that instead of receiving a lump sum, representing his share of a client's first full year of payments, he'd collect incrementally, when the client paid. This was certainly not the way the new rep wanted to do business, and it was an honest mistake on my part. When I realized my error, I felt like I'd discovered a stain on my nice clean shirt, a stain that had been growing without me noticing for some time, and now it was so big, it seemed impossible that I hadn't known it was there all along.

By then, it was too late. The rep had made an exceptional sale and was rightfully expecting a huge upfront payment. If not for that one bad checkmark, his first commission would have broken company records! The situation was serious. I'd hired a sales ace then proceeded to squash his motivation. What would you have done if you'd been in my shoes? I could have tried to deny my fault, to pretend I'd been acting at the rep's direction when I selected the unusual pay style. But that wouldn't have been good for the business. It wouldn't have been the right thing to do. Instead, I went to the rep and apologized. There was no way to correct the mistake retroactively, so while his future payouts were processed the way he wanted, the record-breaking sale never hit the board.

What was the outcome of acting with integrity? First and foremost, I was motivated to learn the intricacies of my job. Never again would I make a seemingly minor mistake that impacted my coworkers' bottom line. The insurance business is complex and confusing, but I became more interested after my error, and in time more knowledgeable. Understanding more about the stakes involved help me avoid future mistakes. As for the sales rep in question, he took the turn of events in stride, commenting that though he'd be collecting upfront for the near future, he'd consider changing his option back later, as it presented an opportunity to save and grow with the company. He knew my reputation, and judged from those in my circle of connections that my error had not been malicious. We were able to move on and work profitably together, which would not have been the case had I failed to own up.

Thanks to the pattern of ethical behavior I'd established, a painful situation turned into a lesson and an opportunity to connect. Having integrity and proving it on a daily basis really does pay off when the chips are down.

A Reality Check

For some years, a department I was a part of operated an ambulance that assisted the local private service. The system seemed to work well, with our EMTs supporting the private entity through the busy times while we continued to focus on fire and rescue. Back in 2010, with budgets tight and funding limited, the department saw an opportunity to take over the city ambulance service, bumping out the private partner. Understand that mandatory overtime is often a necessity in fire departments—when a three-alarm fire is called in, the manpower has to be there—but staffing the ambulance service quickly turned into a nightmare.

The central problem was that the plan that went into effect hadn't been clearly thought out. Used ambulances had to be brought in to fill the gap the private entity had left. We experienced a critical shortage of medics when the changeover happened. At first, interest in learning the skills to help out was high. The bump in pay was minimal but enough to encourage eager beavers. As time passed, however, many lost interest due to the relentless runs and ceaseless overtime EMTs were required to take on. By this phase in the disaster, management's lack of planning had become obvious. Their <u>re</u>active rather than <u>pro</u>active mindset made a deep hole deeper.

Soon, those of us with an interest in the department's well-being noticed the model changing. In addition to emergency runs, ambulances were being called to nonemergent transports. This really should have remained in the purview of the private ambulance service, as vehicles, medics, and drivers were required to remain on-site for extended periods of time while a patient visited a doctor or took medical treatment. From a financial standpoint, this sounded like a great idea to the city, since the patient or their insurance would have to compensate for the time. In practice, it compromised the department's primary mission of responding to emergencies. Maybe the transports could have paid for themselves in time, but with staffing levels low, this was a case of putting the cart before the horse.

On one occasion, I was ordered to shut down the rescue truck in order to drive a patient from the hospital to his house in the standby unit. The patient lived an hour away, and when we got to his apartment, he hopped right out of the bus and skipped to his door. He could've called Uber! After that two-hour diversion, my crew was sent back out to help a lady get her cancer treatment. In total, we spent four hours carting folks around town. I'm always glad to help, but this was four hours our heavy rescue was out of service. Thankfully, none of my family, friends, or anybody else in the community needed rescuing during this period.

What would **U** have done as a city leader, seeing a scenario like this unfold? The path of loyalty, honor, and integrity, to me, is pretty clear. With the existing plan insufficient to meet community needs, the right call would have been to admit that the private ambulance service was a mistake and to call it to the negotiating table. Making such a call would have taken a lot of courage, plus a selfless lack of greed. Sadly, character is not always the first consideration when mistakes are made. It's quite clear, however, that much trouble can be avoided when people set aside the natural impulse to save face.

Since my retirement, I've been told that the transport situation I described above has improved. More people have signed up for medic school, and a balanced approach to staffing has made lives safer. Conditions are more favorable, thanks to these changes. Unfortunately, quite a few good men and women left for other departments during the time of turmoil. Who knows how many VIPs were lost due to a desire to save face?

When your time comes to shine, will you be a lump of coal or a diamond in the rough? Consider this quick list of tips that can help you build rock-solid character:

- Be honest, resisting the impulse to tell "white lies."
- Always fulfill even the smallest promised commitment.
- Let pride in a job well done motivate you to complete routine assignments.
- Keep confidential information to yourself.
- Uproot biased, prejudiced, or vindictive attitudes.
- Don't confuse physical toughness for personal worth.
- Listen to others, especially your fellow firefighters or coworkers.
- If speaking your mind is the right thing to do, bite down and step up.

One of the hardest things for a talented individual to do is bide time waiting for a chance to show their worth. Fear not! By making connections inside the department and outside in the community, you can open up channels for advancement you didn't know existed. Chapter Three: Communication will help you do that.

Flashpoint Review!

- Courage inspires followers and enhances our professionalism.
- People trust leaders who are known for loyalty and selflessness.
- A leader with honor takes decisive action and never brings shame to the organization.

- Nobody's perfect. Integrity moves a VIP to admit mistakes.
- Positional leaders don't always emphasize character. To build influence, **U** must.

Chapter Three: Communication

Communication is essential to make the sort of positive connections that can help you and your organization thrive. If you can learn to make connections with colleagues, superiors, and members of the community, you'll find opportunities to lead become so numerous that you won't have to seek them out. Opportunities and people will come to **U**.

Why do some people have trouble making connections? A few years back, I attended computer programming classes at the house of millionaire Scott Jones, 1150 116th Street, Carmel, Indiana. It was a great experience, where I was introduced to an immersive language-learning curriculum. The teachers at Eleven Fifty Academy, as the school is called, talked a lot about the problems that lack of communication between programmers and management within a company can bring. That's kind of funny if you think about it. Every business these days needs a website, an app, some kind of e-commerce back end. Yet despite the importance of their IT experts, relaying a message from management to programmers is a chore. According to the instructors, the gap the message has to go across might as well be the Grand Canyon.

I found through personal experience that this is true. Trying to communicate with my classmates was as daunting as if I'd just parachuted into the backwoods of a foreign country, whose name I didn't even know! These folks were brilliant at using programming languages to speak to machines, but they came from such niche backgrounds, they couldn't even talk to each other, let alone me, the moonlighting firefighter. Without my instructors to translate, our class would have been left sitting in silence, staring at our laptops.

Similar communication gaps sometimes exist between firefighters and the communities they serve. The section on honor outlined a situation—fighting hot spots after extinguishing a fire—where the thoughts going through a firefighter's mind could damage a department's reputation if they are voiced out loud. Not because the firefighter is thinking anything wrong, mind, but because he or she is speaking from one particular perspective, while those in the community are listening from another. To a greater or lesser extent, differences in perspective affect everybody, whether you're an entrepreneur trying to build a small business or a high-powered exec attempting to grok IT technobabble. How can a leader help the organization interact freely across knowledge gaps?

Reflecting on our Essential Traits will certainly help. We'll be discussing the last five of these traits in detail in the following sections. Delving deep into duty, respect, honesty, genuineness, and empathy will motivate you to want to connect and help broaden your perspective so you'll be able to effectively communicate what you want to say. After you read each subsection, take time to recall a time when you made a connection with someone using the trait discussed, or one when you missed an opportunity to connect because you lacked strength in that trait.

If you're a person who struggles with communication, don't worry. It's never too late to learn! As your network of connections diversifies, you'll find yourself excelling as a communicator. It may even become the strength **U** are famous for.

Duty

Duty motivates us to train hard and do our best. For firefighters, that means protecting the lives and property of those in the communities we serve. Firefighters' courage is celebrated in many different ways in the American culture, but many don't appreciate the selflessness necessary to make a career out of putting your own life on the line for others. That's okay. Firefighters don't serve for recognition. They make a commitment and take pride in measuring up. Whether your job is building bridges or selling apples at a roadside stand, to be a VIP, **U** can do no less.

A successful leader doesn't meet only the minimum standard; they strive to always be their best. Duty can be measured by initiative. Do you anticipate needs and do what has to be done without being told? That's a sign that your sense of duty surpasses head knowledge. Leading requires initiative. Very Influential People have purpose; they go beyond simply caring for directed tasks. Being proactive, they set an example of conscientiousness, thoroughness, and reliability, even when mentally and physically exhausted. Every follower who imitates that example is a connection, a boost to the leader's influence.

If you want to be a leader others will happily follow, then competence, attention to detail, and sensitivity to the needs of the team must always be a priority. These qualities are developed through balanced learning, self-improvement, realistic training, and professional experience, all of which trace back to initiative. Do you look for ways to practice skills and be a good example during your time off? If you are in a leadership role already, do you help others improve by assigning confidence-building tasks? Look for opportunities to challenge yourself and those you work with. If you don't push yourself, you'll never progress. If you don't push others, what is influence for?

Some people don't have the desire to connect. They go about their business day after day—same old, same old. They don't feel the urge to change, the drive to learn and grow. They're not interested in refining themselves as influential leaders. Those who are positional leaders are willfully stuck where seniority or necessity put them. Even if they can see the importance of connecting, they don't want to put in the work.

I'm going to make a statement that might be controversial, but please hear me out. Not everybody can be a leader. I don't mean that some people are incapable of cultivating the traits I've outlined. Some simply don't have the drive. Drive is the first possession any VIP needs, transcending all others. It's the desire to connect.

Interestingly, the desire to connect is a drive we're all born with. Think about it: How long would you have lived if you hadn't connected with Mom, Dad, or some other caregiver at birth? Yet, despite this promising start, many of us decide at some point in life that we're better off trying to make decisions to satisfy only ourselves, to isolate ourselves, be our own judge and jury, the captain of our own ship.

I once had this attitude. In my military and professional career, a desire to connect was something I had to rediscover. I knew from the first that I wanted to be a leader, but I didn't know that leading meant making connections. Due to poor examples and personal choices, I got off on the wrong foot, thinking that leading meant giving orders. Only later did I learn that a leader must inspire others, to make them want to follow. Leadership is influence, pure and simple. Having learned that lesson, I made a decision to change, and started on a path to doing my duty better than ever before.

We're going to delve deeper into communication traits than we did with character, partly because so many struggle with communicating, but mostly because the lessons I've learned in this area have been so hard won. We'll explore each trait in three subsections. In this section, we'll explore why duty Is Important Off the Job. We'll talk about how it Motivates **U** to Think Long Term. And we'll detail how duty Helps **U** Connect with Your Team. You may want to skip ahead to this section's Flashpoint Review! in order to fix in your mind the key points you'll want to watch for.

. . . Is Important Off the Job

Duty doesn't begin and end with response to a crisis. Day-to-day operations provide leaders opportunities to assess and improve their skills. That means seeking out fellow VIPs, asking questions, even requesting performance critiques. These are all great opportunities to connect.

A common misconception is that duty applies only on the job. Adopting that attitude can tear down the influence you've built. Teammates see us at our best and at our worst. Demonstrating that we're serious about duty even when we're relaxing or working a job on the side keeps the message clear and consistent.

How can communicating affect your side work? Regardless of whether you do manual labor or practice brain surgery in your spare time, the connections you develop can make or break your business. Providing clients a positive experience will lead to genuine satisfaction, both for clients and yourself. Happy clients will advertise for you. We all know that bad reports spread like wildfire, but positive feedback takes time to bear fruit. Like a tree, it has to push down roots before it can grow up and out. Every time you put shine and uniqueness into your business, you deepen those roots.

Firefighters typically work a days-on/days-off schedule, so many of us seek opportunities to earn extra income. I often ask firefighters struggling to build a business if they are receiving referrals. If not, I ask why they think no one is telling others about their lawn or roofing service, or whatever. Could it be that they're not communicating? Perhaps they're not showing that they value their clients by going the extra mile.

My follow-up question sometimes takes them by surprise. "When was the last time you referred somebody to one of your clients?" I say.

If this is a new concept to you, take a moment to pull out your client list. Everybody on there has a skill. Does a guy you cut lawns for paint houses on the side? When was the last time you sent him work? Where side jobs are concerned, firefighters try to spread the money around. A guy on A-shift may cut a B-shift guy's yard. We all expect to get paid back for referrals, but what about paying forward? To get, first you must give, without expecting anything in return. The power of this principle has been attested by leaders around the world. It's even in the Bible!

Let's get real here. Everybody is selling. We're selling ourselves, our ideas, our hopes, and our dreams every day. When you talk about your business, you're doing more than selling what you do. You're selling **U**. Learning to communicate and connect will build the rapport you need to be successful. My family often rags on me about the deep conversations I get into when I meet new people. I admit, some of these can run quite long. Mostly, though, the conversations aren't about me. I listen, show a genuine interest, and ask questions to show I want to learn more. Over the years, I've made some extremely valuable connections this way, connections that have paid me back socially, financially, and professionally. The skills I developed through connecting helped me do my duty as an active firefighter. Today, they continue to help me serve firefighters and police officers as a Midwest manager for Police and Fire Insurance.

. . . Motivates U to Think Long Term

One vital lesson I have learned about doing my duty is the importance of thinking ahead. If you discount people for the little they've achieved so far, you can miss out on connections later that you'll kick yourself for not making. In the same way VIPs should not underestimate their own potential, don't underestimate others, either. You never know, years in the future, who may be on the other side of the negotiating table during a union contract or sitting in a council seat during budget time. How much better would you feel walking into a contract meeting if you found that the chairperson was a client of your lawn care business, or the secretary's daughter used to babysit your kids?

Institutionally speaking, a fire department has to think about the effects community connections will have in ten or twenty years. Taking a short-term view can lead to long-term problems. Years ago, my former department agreed with city leaders to stagger negotiations by separating concerns into two different packages. One year, we'd meet to discuss wage adjustments. The next year, we'd tackle working conditions. The benefit of this arrangement was supposed to be quicker turnaround times, plus fewer delays on implementing contracts. In practice, every year was a race against the clock. Often, wage negotiations would spill over into the next year, disrupting our working conditions. Because the negotiators couldn't see past the immediate problems, they were unable to move on. Tension got high and little was gained.

Splitting the negotiation period wasn't the only cause of frustration. I often thought that our negotiators could have made the system work if only they'd had deeper connections with city leaders. Of course, it takes time to build connections like that. Things could have been so much smoother if the negotiators had been proactive, seeking out ways to connect with future leaders, back when they were young firefighters, new to the department. That would have required a long-term view.

Sometimes opportunities to connect come along when you're not looking. Back in 1993, when I was working in the service department at Cellular One, a temporary hire came in to handle our phone traffic. She was polite and made friends easily. I don't remember how long she worked at the front desk, but I had learned enough about leadership at that point not to underestimate the value of a connection. Twenty years later, that former part-time employee was sitting on city council in my city, making decisions that affected the fire department. Not long after, I met a sixteen-year-old kid shopping for his first cell phone. He impressed me—it's not that often you meet a young person who really knows where they're going in life. Each time this kid came in, he was friendly and communicative, demonstrating a gift-of-the-gab I admired. Within the past decade, he has emerged as a top realtor in my area. A mover and a shaker, his influence within the community is considerable. I'm glad I took the chance to get to know him when I did.

If you struggle to connect with people as I did, don't give up! You can overcome the communication barrier by reaching out to different kinds of people: young, old, those with position and/or influence, and those without. An easy way to start is by improving your communication skills with those you're comfortable with already. Who in your extended family has shown an interest in what you do?

Can you take an interest in their work, maybe help them reach their ambitions? What are they hoping to achieve in three years, five years, ten? Think about your training. You've dealt with situations that are unique to your field. What can **U** teach somebody close to you that they won't have heard elsewhere? So-called common knowledge is often anything but. You'd be amazed at the positive connections you can make by relating simple truths.

It takes years, sometimes decades, to build connections of high value. Many opportunities are lost by people and organizations that take a short-term view. Don't make the same mistake.

. . . Helps U Connect with Your Team

One of the most important duties of a leader is to provide a clear path to accomplish the mission. In the communication context, a clear path means the ability to convey purpose, vision, and goals to your team. This is a unique quality. It can't be replaced by anything else.

Years ago, I had a lieutenant who was an extremely hard worker. He'd entered the fire service at an older age, after experience in the military and the working world. The sweat he put into every job was impressive and a frequent topic of conversation. In contrast with his intense physical effort, his communication skills were lacking. I don't mean the guy didn't know how to talk. It's just that sometimes he concentrated so much on his part of the task at hand that he forget to give instruction to anybody else. Instead of building a strong team, his approach was to grab a line and charge ahead. He led by example, but only by example. At times, this would even make him skimp on evaluating his own situation.

The most vivid example in my mind happened during a structure fire. The lieutenant's blinders were on and, as occasionally happened, the team lost touch with him. When the time came for us to take on new assignments, we hunted around and saw him hauling an inch-and-three-quarter attack line into the structure. Just as we were moving his way, he opened the bail, aiming to knock down fire heading for an exposure. The water shot out so hard he started to spin. He literally spun in circles because of the water pressure. I honestly don't know if I've ever seen anything funnier. Still, it wasn't a very effective way to fight the fire.

In emergency situations, communicating with others can make or break your success. Effective communication with the team is essential in other areas, too. It builds credibility inside and out, deepening positive associations and trust.

Of equal importance, communicating with the team fosters cooperation. An excellent example of cooperation that I've had the privilege of visiting as an insurance representative is Brookville Fire Department in Brookville, Ohio. A small, two-station department, it houses both volunteer and part-time firefighters. Part of its strength is that most of those part-timers are career firefighters moonlighting from other departments. Those who aren't are looking to start a career.

The men and women of Brookville surround themselves with hardworking individuals. They favor those who are friendly, funny, and not afraid to connect. Chief Ron Fletcher understands the strengths of everybody on his team and brings out the best in each one. He and his crew have built an atmosphere of trust and encouragement. They're like a family. Every time I stop in to check on their members, I get a sense of the closeness of their connections. They even make me feel like part of the team! There's never a question, at a department like Brookville, about who's going to get an invitation to a Christmas party. When the part-timers run into a volunteer at K's Restaurant or Great Wall, they stop and say hello.

Connections like Brookville's don't just happen. They're the result of team building, VIPs making an effort to bring everyone together to achieve a goal.

What can **U** do to enrich the environment of your department? Think about the pitfalls you could help a new recruit avoid by helping her chart a clear path. If you're just starting out in your own career, imagine the benefits of connecting with experienced members of your team. However heavy your duties are now, you'll find them easier to carry when you work closely with others.

Flashpoint Review!

- Do your duty off the job by paying contacts forward.
- You never know how valuable a connection might turn out to be, so it's important to think long term.
- Present followers a clear path to doing their duty. You're all in this together!

Respect

Having **respect** helps us communicate patiently and avoid becoming insensitive to other people's concerns. This is especially true for firefighters, military personnel, and police, who often deal with people who are having the worst day of their lives. In all walks of life, respect reminds us to make allowances for people's behavior when they are facing day-to-day hardships. Leaders show respect by connecting visually, giving others their undivided attention. Since the eyes are the windows of the soul, the sense of purpose that informs everything **U** do will show in your eyes.

When you connect with someone, you show that you respect their purpose. In turn, they'll respect yours, not because you're entitled to their respect, but because you bring value they're looking for. It's like I always tell my kids, "Education may get you in the front door, but it's the things not taught in school—personality, work ethic, drive, energy, character—that will make you successful." The way others perceive you is a vital component of that success. The key to making that perception favorable is respect.

Why do some elevated to a position of leadership command respect, while others do not? The leader who doesn't give respect will never get it. Remember, you must give first. Think about the last time you were in a meeting, receiving training for some upcoming task. Did you make it a point to look eager? Were you enthusiastic to learn? If so, your trainer no doubt felt your energy. So did fellow trainees.

You demonstrated respect for everybody's time and attention. Did they give it back?

During my first year with the fire service, I was called out to a fire at a local factory. An off-balance trailer had elevated the bed of a truck, causing it to contact power lines. Upon arrival, I stood at a distance while Acting Lieutenant Tim Brown observed a large arc running from the semi to contact the ground below. Between the fuel tank of the truck and a large transformer lay the driver. He was a man my own age, I later found out. He had been electrocuted when the bed had contacted. His body was bouncing as the charge ran through it.

We couldn't do anything until the electricity was turned off. Standing around, waiting, went against my every impulse. I hated not being able to move the victim's body or take action to control the blaze. In this difficult situation, the leadership Tim showed was outstanding. As a driver engineer, he took command in the absence of a senior officer, demonstrating the value of his experience. If Tim hadn't been there, I could easily imagine a young firefighter like I was getting so focused on the victim that he made himself a part of the problem instead of the solution. Despite his own struggle to contain impatience, Tim calmly laid out our plan while we waited for confirmation from the company that the power had been disconnected.

Once we got the green light, I hit the fire, soaking the gas tanks while Tim dragged the victim clear. His levelheadedness was admirable, but not unusual in Tim. It was typical of the strengths he showed as he rose through the ranks to assistant chief. I cheered every step of his advancement. The confidence he had in his own abilities and the confidence he showed in mine over the years made him easy to respect.

When we lack respect for the people we work with, teamwork is a chore, and communication feels like something we want to flee from, rather than pursue. Having respect for others, as well as ourselves, can get us through some tough situations. Still, respect doesn't come automatically. You have to put work into it, but believe me, it Pays Out What **U** Put In. When situations come along that don't go our way, respect Helps **U** Stay Positive. And when we're tempted to rush through our busy schedules, a habit that can tempt us to blow people off, respect Conveys Interest in Others. In the following sections, we'll show by example that all these statements are true.

. . . Pays Out What U Put In

I've always been something of a musician. Early in my firefighting career, I played the critter circuit in a band called Backdraft. It was a great experience, but after several years I felt like I needed something more than playing in smoky halls to the same faces. I had mixed feelings about moving on, but on my thirtieth birthday, I had an experience that crystallized everything. My wife and I were on a weekend trip to Nashville. During our two-night stay I caught a break, performing with the house band at Legends Lounge. As I left that evening, the bartender said, "You're the Singing Fireman from Indiana, right? Great job tonight." By the time I got back from the trip I'd decided to roll my modest celebrity into a business.

I started a website, www.thesingingfireman.com, and resigned from the band. I wasn't planning to mortgage the house to cut a demo or anything, I just felt I could build my business by concentrating on solo gigs. I wanted to find a style that would make me stand out from the crowd. It didn't take me long to figure out that venues will hire a musician back not based on talent or song choices, but if the money is good at the end of the night.

My solo gigs usually lasted four hours, with three ten-minute breaks, one after every hour of playing. Tips were encouraged, but if you're basically singing to yourself, the tips don't come in, and the bar doesn't rake in the cash. I noticed that I was losing people during my breaks, in bigger chunks as the night wore on, so to keep the audience engaged, I added a few features to my performances. During the breaks, I played upbeat music, something different from my own selections. That gave people a chance to refresh their senses while still keeping them entertained.

After some experimentation, I began matching people up in a minute-to-win-it game, some physical challenge using props on hand. I typically chose players from larger groups, then bought both players a drink of their choice. My thinking was that if I treated both winner and loser, the fair-minded loser's friends would pony up for the winning table's next round. This strategy worked like gangbusters, bringing both the bars and me extra income. I kept up my singing and deejaying, and at the end of my night, 80% of the early crowd was still present, drinking, and engaged.

My gigs were fun and popular, thanks in large part to the extra effort I put in. Now, I know what you're thinking. What do my bar games have to do with respect? Well, think about my motivation. As much as I enjoy playing music, these gigs were for the audience, not myself. They were the folks I was trying to reach. Respecting my craft helped me want to give my all. Respecting my audience helped me devise ways to keep them happy. This can be true in your business, too. Is there an ordinary activity **U** engage in, be it a side job, hobby, or something else, that you could add fun and excitement to? You might be surprised how much going the extra mile can improve your personal life and professional career.

. . . Helps U Stay Positive

Giving respect isn't always easy. It takes energy, time, and a willingness to open your mind. You have to build a desire to get to know other people and view them in a positive light. People who pursue leadership tend to be highly driven. We want to go above and beyond, yet a whole lot of people seem to want to hold us back. Positional leaders don't always know what we're capable of, so we wind up wasting a lot of breath asking them to let go of our shirttails so we can run. Showing respect for authority figures who put us in this stuck state requires that we work hard to see every challenge in a positive light.

How can you remain positive when leadership is holding you back? Remember that in making your personal progress toward leadership, influence is what's important. As John C. Maxwell says, "Leadership is influence, nothing more, nothing less." The myopic positional leaders who don't want to hear your innovative ideas are not, in the long run, going to be able to hinder you from connecting in the organization and the wider world. They're probably not even going to recognize what you're doing as you build influence and give respect so you can give it back.

How can **U** use influence to grow? Again, you have to commit to going the extra mile. VIPs lead by example. We're good role models, committed to making the best of every situation. Taking a long-term view, we make time to help others. One great example of this is my former supervisor, Bobby Farris. Bobby was deputy chief of fire prevention in Richmond, Indiana, and an icon from the day he entered the fire service to the day he left. Bobby was never too busy, too proud, or too worn out to engage with the community. He delivered outstanding customer service and let people know he cared. As a fire marshal, he not only treated businesspeople professionally, but also trained kids, from preschoolers to high school seniors, on the importance of fire prevention.

I remember many times we worked together on a program. Bobby had a way of connecting with kids and parents that was a joy to behold. His impact on the community is still felt today. Students he taught now tell their kids and grandkids about the positive influence Bobby Farris had on their lives. Years after his retirement, Bobby and I remain close friends.

One truth Bobby understood in his career is that the city we work for and the fire department we work in will never be able to accomplish their mission unless the leaders and firefighters are on the same page.

Respecting one another plays a huge role. Imagine a group of frat house boys playing tug-of-war against a team of firefighters. I don't care if the firefighters' anchor man is a twenty-year vet with blown-out knees. My money is still on our guys dragging the loudmouths into the mud. Firefighters know how to pull a line, but more importantly, they know how to pull together. Teamwork is going to win every time, provided the team is united.

Can you bring that same sort of unity to understanding others, giving respect, and communicating the purpose that drives **U** to succeed? An organization with vision develops its leaders. To accomplish its mission, it works to support VIPs in their efforts at personal advancement. From longtime veterans down to new recruits, everybody has a contribution to make. Never forget, whether your job is to manage a shift or to sweep up the floors, the mission of the organization can only be accomplished if you do your best. Respecting your team enough to put in the needed work is critical. You'll be surprised by how much influence **U** can gain by delivering consistent effort with a positive attitude.

. . . Conveys Interest in Others

Respect gets at the core of communication, expressing your interest in other people. To phrase it another way, respect shows you like someone. It takes effort to show interest in different types of people, but you don't have to be a loudmouth or party animal to successfully connect. Believe it or not, you can be an introvert and still come across as an extrovert. Consider Elvis Presley. One of the most famous entertainers in history, he kept to himself when not in the public eye. Elvis could turn on the charm like a light switch. When he was on stage, he epitomized devotion to his craft and respect for his fans.

We live in an impatient world. People get upset when you don't respond immediately to a text message. They lean on their horns if you don't push the gas fast enough on a green light. The majority of people have problems with communicating and connecting with others. Speed is the problem. Sometimes, to speed up, **U** first have to slow down. Slowing down helps in all aspects of communication. It shows the interest you have for others and demonstrates respect for both them and yourself.

We all know people who act like they're hopped up on a gallon of caffeine. They zip around like hummingbirds, always on a mission. Getting to know such busy folks is tough because they never have time to talk. They're wound so tight, they've got to spin their wheels or explode. I've had days when I was cranked like that. You tend to miss the little things, sometimes the big things, too. I've been so consumed by my own spinning thoughts at times that I've walked right by people without acknowledging their existence. A bad habit that I've been working on is that when I'm speaking to a couple, I sometimes speak to the person I know and walk away immediately after, not even saying "hi" to the other person. I'm sure I've missed out on many excellent conversations and several valuable connections by being in a rush.

To accomplish anything of value, you have to learn to intentionally manage your energy. Athletes, performers, and professional speakers are great examples of this. They know that if they don't pace themselves properly, they won't get results. According to business trainer Clancy Cross, "People often confuse energy with volume or speed. An accomplished musician knows that it requires more energy to sing or play slowly and softly, to connect with the audience, than it does to race and blast away. Even the way we sit with people and listen to them requires energy." He concludes, "You can't fake energy and you can't fake a connection."[2]

How do you stop yourself from blazing past people with barely a thought? Train yourself to do your best at communicating, just as you train to do your best at your paid job. Consider the following training tips for communicating with individuals, groups, and your community. Don't be discouraged if an exercise doesn't come easily at first. Take your time, and follow the advice. As your appreciation for other people grows, you'll naturally learn to respect them more. You'll find yourself seeking out helpful, lasting connections.

COMMUNICATING WITH INDIVIDUALS

- Don't get lazy with your listening skills. Always portray a sense of interest. Use active listening techniques, such as maintaining eye contact and asking clarifying questions, to make the other person feel important.
- Don't take for granted that people want to hear your opinions. Be available to hear theirs first. As your connection develops, they'll let you know when your input is welcome.

- Work at increasing your energy. Get enthusiastic about what the other person is saying. If you're not feeling recharged but still value the connection, fake it 'til you make it.
- Be mentally prepared to learn. Soak up words like a sponge. You can decide later if what you absorbed is worth preserving or should be squeezed out.
- Be emotionally available. Nothing will destroy a connection faster than holding somebody at a distance when they're asking to get closer. I don't mean this in a romantic sense, though the advice works there, too. Every connection you make requires both parties to trust each other a little more than they did before. If somebody is telling you about their business plans or their hopes to enter public office, and you don't show excitement, any chance you had to form an alliance is gone, maybe for good.

COMMUNICATING IN A GROUP

- Remember that those in your audience are human. Their attention level will vary with their energy. If you're slinging new ideas to them at the end of a busy shift, are they going to be at their most receptive? If you can't choose a better time, you'll need to generate enthusiasm. Complacency is the idea killer.
- If you're meeting your audience for the first time, introduce yourself to as many individuals as possible before you address the group. Ask each person you meet a question to uncover their uniqueness.

- Give those you meet ownership of the conversation by answering their questions.
- When the discussion begins, draw in those who are hesitant by acknowledging their strengths. For instance, you may need "young blood" to bring new ideas, or "seasoned pros" to share the benefit of their experience. Everybody has something to offer.
- Always end your talk by asking the group how you can help them be successful.

COMMUNICATING WITH THE COMMUNITY

- Connect with passion. Don't be afraid of your enthusiasm; embrace it!

- Be positive. Every challenge can be overcome if enough of the right people confront it.

- Prepare well in advance. Know who will be in your audience, whether few or many. Predicting exactly the individuals you might interact with at an emergency scene or a public hearing is impossible, so prepare answers for the type of people you're likely to meet. Make sure these answers convey empathy and engagement.

- Give of yourself. In whatever situation you find yourself communicating, be ready to be a source of energy, in addition to the passion, positivity, and respect you'll be putting out. When you meet people at their worst, be at your best.

- As above, connect with people by understanding how their uniqueness relates to your mission. Show respect to help them help you.

Flashpoint Review!

- Use your unique talents to add a little extra to what you do. You'll be surprised at the connections you can strengthen.
- Have the vision to maintain a positive outlook. Nobody can hold you back from being an influencer.
- Show respect to others, and ask their help in achieving your goals.

Honesty and Genuineness

One important benefit of **honesty** is that it helps us see situations for what they are. Think about a time when you failed to meet some goal. I'm not talking about an emergency situation, where many conditions are out of our control. Think more in terms of a meeting you attended or a negotiation whose outcome was important to you. Perhaps you were asking for a raise in salary or were tasked with helping put together a budget. You knew going in that good sense was on your side. You deserved the increase or had a case to make for every penny the upcoming project would cost. Your boss or your colleagues would be fools not to listen, you thought. And yet, all you got for your trouble was a fight and a headache. Your audience didn't listen. You might as well have been talking to a wall.

It's tempting to blame a failure like that on the folks across the table, but the fact is, breakdowns like this arise when you, as the negotiator, don't have enough influence to sway your audience. Do you see the role honesty plays? Instead of blaming others for what happened, an honest person will ask: What could I have done better? Would some other line of reasoning have produced a better outcome?

Without honesty to slap us around, it's all too easy to deny our need for personal growth, rendering such growth impossible. We can't control other people, only seek to be a positive influence. If we're honest, though, we can control our own behavior. Honesty of this sort has a close relationship with **genuineness**. A genuine person doesn't shirk responsibility. Their motivations show on the surface and run bone deep. We've all dealt with people who are less than genuine. They say one thing and mean something else. The more they tell you they're sincere, the harder it is to believe they're speaking from the heart.

Honesty is essential if you want to be genuine. Genuineness is essential to communication. Taken together, these traits Open **U** Up to Connecting. They Show **U** Value Others. When you're trying to do your best and do your duty, honesty and genuineness Remind **U** To Listen. They truly are must-haves for a VIP!

. . . Opens U Up to Connecting

One of the most common communication barriers can also be the one that's hardest to confront. Simply put, that barrier is openness, how we answer the question, "Will I let people into my life?"

Connecting with family, friends, community, or coworkers is a two-way street. We can't expect people to tell us their private thoughts and genuine concerns if we hold back from giving them the same about ourselves. This is yet another area where you've got to give to receive. Often, negative life experiences make us want to close off, shutting other people out of our inner world. We don't want to let anyone inside. Letting others get to know us feels like giving them power to hurt or manipulate.

Inside the walls of the firehouse, nothing is sacred. If you open your mouth too wide, you're liable to stick your foot in it, and voicing touchy-feely emotions can be taken as an invitation for jibes and snickers (not the candy bar). Think for a moment, though, about the influential leaders you've come across. Whether you're picturing an old boss, a fire chief, military commander, coach, teacher, pastor, or your own parent, that leader let you know where you stood. When you walked up, they'd give you a look, a smile, a nod, or a shake of the head. Sometimes they'd take a knee with you, break down what it was they expected to see that day/month/year. If you genuinely listened, they told you how they felt. You might not have known their politics, but you knew when they were happy about what was happening where the rubber met the road.

My junior high football coach, Bill Dean, was a genuinely good guy. He was also a marine, so not exactly one of those "sensitive types" you read about in magazines. I remember when he first came to our school, when I was in seventh grade. I went up to him and told him I was going to be his quarterback next year. He smirked and said, "We'll see."

Coach Dean was a motivator. Losing wasn't part of his game plan. He was intimidating, with a mug like a bulldog. When Coach Dean was running practice, the team worked harder than during the games themselves. I, my brother Bruce, and our halfback friends drilled handoffs and options so much that we could fake defenders in our sleep. Before every game, Coach Dean cued up "Eye of the Tiger" on cassette tape. After our victories, he'd play "We Are the Champions." He didn't have to switch up the routine. Our whole first year under his coaching, the team went undefeated.

When I was a senior in high school, Bruce and I went to visit Bill Dean. We told him we had enlisted in the army and our plans to leave immediately after graduation. He said, "You guys will never make it." Coming from somebody else, I might have dismissed that comment as rude or just negative, but Coach Dean had a way of getting his point across. Any time he busted our ***ahem*** self-confidence, what he was really saying was, "I believe you can do it. Show me I'm right." Even when his mouth was saying something different, his body language and tough-guy stare told us to take on the challenge like the fighters he taught us to be.

The point is that you don't have to be a gusher to be honest and genuine with people. You can be open without talking strangers through your life story. Coach Dean was not as open an individual as I, personally, try to be. Think of his example as the "you must be this tall to ride" sign outside a roller coaster. The least you can do on your way to connecting with others is to express your expectations genuinely; emphasis on "least." The more open the book of your life is, the more folks will be inclined to read it.

Many people put up a shield after being lied to by people they trusted. I used to work with detectives investigating arson cases.

Frequently, we'd perform neighborhood canvasses. Sometimes I'd sit in on interviews with witnesses, or even suspects, at police headquarters. If the person we talked to was a habitual offender, they were usually close-mouthed. The same was true of those who came from dysfunctional homes. In contrast, people from stable households who'd never been in serious trouble with the law would usually open up after a few minutes of questioning.

The difference isn't hard to understand. People from the first group had been burned, if you'll pardon that expression. They'd been wronged by family members, those they thought were friends, or law enforcement officials they'd encountered previously. They weren't about to trust me or my fellow investigators. Their personal experience taught the lesson, true or not, that the majority of individuals will use and abuse. They'd learned not to take a friend's word, let alone a stranger's. Understanding that helped me have patience during interviews. I learned that with time, even the most insurmountable obstacles can be worked around.

The fact is, connecting with people who have shut themselves off emotionally takes time and effort. If you shut yourself off, connecting becomes impossible. Only by being honestly and genuinely open can you break down this major barrier to communication.

. . . Shows U Value Others

One reason we sometimes fail to connect is that we have an inflated sense of our own importance. We feel that our own opinions are more valuable than those of the people around us. An overinflated ego can easily create a barrier between ourselves and our teammates. It can quickly lead us to undervalue others more distant from us in the organization—even our superiors—and people in the community at large. Note that the motivation to improve in this area can be said to derive from any number of traits we've already discussed, including selflessness, honor, duty, and respect. It's in the moment, when we're face-to-face with an audience, that honesty and genuineness can carry the day.

Consider some of the ways that **U** can show that you value others.

VALUING OTHERS ONE-ON-ONE

- Ask yourself, "How do others make me feel valued?" Can you imitate their example?
- Be a good listener.
- Ask questions about why they value the things they do.
- Share values that are similar to theirs.
- Work together on skills that support your common goals.

VALUING THE ORGANIZATION AS A WHOLE

- Participate in group training and activities. Use enthusiasm to lead by example.
- Recognize that the majority almost always knows better than the individual. Even when the individual knows better, insisting on doing things their way usually does more harm than good.
- Discover individual strengths within the group.
- Acknowledge each person's contribution and potential.

- Encourage input. Where possible, allow people to lead in their area of strength.

VALUING ORGANIZATION AND COMMUNITY LEADERS

- Personally and publicly express your appreciation for the services they provide.
- Look for something special you can do for them. How could you use your spare time to benefit them or their employees?
- Don't overlook quiet people. They're often the deepest thinkers.
- Make eye contact, looking at each person in a way that signals that they are the most important person at the present time.
- Always finish a conversation by thanking the leader for taking time to speak.

Consider the effect these suggestions can have on your relationships if you apply them honestly and with genuineness. It's easy to pretend interest in a given subject. We've all met the guy who thinks he can tell us how to do our job because his uncle held a similar position for five minutes back in the eighties. Mostly, guys like that are harmless. But we don't generally credit them with honesty or genuineness. We don't feel valued in their conversation. If we connect, it's in spite of, not thanks to their attitude. By genuinely valuing the contributions of others, we can make meaningful, lasting connections.

. . . Reminds **U** *to Listen*

I met Sheriff Jeff Cappa years ago while he was working at Sears part time. My soon-to-be wife happened to also be working at Sears, in the shoe department. Sheriff Cappa looked out for her, acting as a father figure. Always approachable, he's the type of guy who, whenever I ran into him, always graciously gave his time to ask about the family. On a few occasions, I saw him at chamber of commerce events. I could tell he was a "mover and a shaker," making connections up, down, and sideways with community leaders. He made it a point to visit everyone he knew at every event, which kept him on the hop for the duration.

During parades and other functions, he was always in a friendly, positive mood. I remember when I took over as department representative for Police and Firemen's Insurance, he gave me the most precious thing he could, a hearing ear. Sheriff Cappa listened to how enrollment could benefit his officers. He understood the importance of making officers aware of their eligibility for these benefits. After our talk, he kindly reassured me of his support.

"Brian," he said, "let me know what you need and when you'd like to talk. Call me on my personal phone."

I don't think he realized the impact he had on me. For more than twenty years, he's been a role model, helping me understand the importance of communicating to connect. Among the lessons I learned from him is the importance of genuinely listening to perspectives different from my own. Listening, as Sheriff Cappa could tell you, opens opportunities for lifelong relationships. As I think back on our interactions, I'm humbled by the time this busy man was willing to spend with me. Our encouraging conversations have made our relationship stronger.

Are there people in your community you can point to as exemplary listeners? Connecting in this way can be a challenge. Consider the difficulty 9-1-1 dispatchers face when speaking to callers over the phone. Without a visual to go by, the only clues they have to the urgency of a situation are the words, tone of voice, and urgency of the caller, occasionally assisted by background noise. Those who haven't had the experience of speaking to a civilian at the peak of stress might think that the words should be enough. In a time crunch, where seconds count, dispatchers have to go beyond words, listening to (and through) the underlying emotions.

Just as the quality of the signal can make or break an emergency call, everything **U** do when speaking has the potential to enhance or degrade the quality of the signal you're putting out. When the other person is talking, it's vital to let them go at their own pace, using audible and visual cues to understand how they are feeling. Consider the following phrase:

"I can't take it anymore!"

Without knowing the context, can you imagine the different tones of voice an individual might use when saying those words? Suppose the speaker was a victim of domestic abuse or was telling you about a violent confrontation that happened in her neighborhood. Her tone would reflect a number of negative emotions.

But what if you overheard that same individual at a comedy club, delivering the same line after laughing at some hilarious zinger? Would you expect to hear the same tone? Context can act as a modifier of emotional content, even when the words remain the same. So to listen with genuine interest, you have to pay attention to more than words.

One more point on honest listening before we move on: Interacting with people inside and outside of your organization is not always going to be sunshine and rainbows. Occasionally, you'll have to take out the trash. If a person with whom you're speaking is combative, it's important to use your listening skills to find out quickly what personality type they are, then defuse the situation.

Are they the sort who will settle down if you show a calm demeanor? Or will they raise their intensity, trying to make you react? A certain subset of people talk big because they like to be heard. Another subset wants to get you mad so they can justify their temper. A third type, one you see a lot in the military, is those who will push your buttons purely as a test to see if you'll stand up for yourself.

Listening for the difference can turn a bad situation into a positive example for your teammates, even if the blowhard giving you grief isn't impressed. Honesty and genuineness are critical here. You've got to be genuinely calm, if the speaker responds well to calm. If they're looking to stir the pot, you've got to be honest in any answers you give, since the goal of the individual may be to later get you in trouble for something you said. If an aggressor is looking to push your buttons and you've already done everything you can to keep a lid on the situation, you'll have to be brutally honest when calling their bluff. If you measure your words, speak genuinely, and don't exaggerate, eyewitnesses to the confrontation will take your side.

It's not always possible to smooth over anger on the spot. Sometimes you've got to do your best, then move on. Listening for the cues in the other person's voice will equip **U** to answer in the best way you can. Maybe you'll even be able to connect with someone who observed your smart handling of the situation.

Flashpoint Review!

- Be honest with yourself and you'll want to connect with others.
- Genuine communicating protects you from developing an inflated opinion of yourself.
- Listening skills are critical to resolving hostile situations.

Empathy

Empathy, defined as showing interest in understanding others, is both a motivating factor for our wanting to connect and a key to communicating what we want to say effectively. Empathy allows us to step outside of ourselves and see the world through somebody else's eyes. If **U** can master empathy, you'll have little trouble forming deep, long-lasting connections.

Many problems in people's lives come from a failure of empathy—divorce, estrangement, as well as every kind of crime—that it deserves looking into on its own merits. The role empathy plays in communication, however, makes it easy to see how putting in the work to learn empathy will pay off. Empathy is invaluable to a communicator and VIP. Being able to relate to others' feelings Connects **U** with Your Audience. When facing an audience you're not sure will be receptive, empathy Breaks Down Defensive Attitudes. When the audience is inclined to listen, it's because your empathy Speaks to Minds and Hearts. Read on to learn how **U** can connect with empathy.

. . . Connects U with Your Audience

Here's another gem from John C. Maxwell: "Words are the currency of ideas and have the power to change the world." How true that is! People can respond positively or negatively to your choice of words. While it's true that our actions speak more loudly, how many folks are actually around to see us in action? A firefighter's boldest actions take place out of the public eye. When I'm helping insurance clients cover their hospital bills, much of the work I do on their behalf takes place alone in my office. As much as we want to show others we care, situations often require that we tell them what they missed. It's vital, then, to use our words in a way that will emphasize positive qualities like honor and integrity. By doing so we can increase influence and strengthen personal bonds.

While the right words are important, the way we deliver those words can turn a dry, uninteresting speech into a memorable occasion for a fascinated audience. Have you ever been the guy who forgot to silence his phone during a lecture from a superior? A call comes in, you scramble to cut the sound before the boss pinpoints where it's coming from, and all along you're thinking that the speech you're hearing is so dry, you'd rather take the call. Maybe you've gone over the material in the lecture so often that you don't feel you need a reminder. More likely, it's the delivery, the presentation of the material, that's failed to hold your interest.

How can **U** make your own presentations engaging to those who listen? Well, what holds your interest in a speech? Here are three keys to fascinating delivery.

BE POSITIVE

Being negative is easy. There's always something to complain about. Your department is missing its training goals. You're doing your best on a slashed budget. You're working with a skeleton crew.

The audience knows how bad things are. It's your job to be the ray of hope that makes the naysayers believe in possibilities. You can meet next month's goals—you will! Your department is a tight ship—you'll make that budget stretch! The crew you're left with is the best of the best!

When your team succeeds, praise them. When they fall a little short, give credit for what they did right while advising on what needs improvement. Personalize your positive reinforcement. Don't be fake. Even green recruits can spot insincerity.

Set a goal to show positive examples, even in the most difficult circumstances. The brave men and women who charged into the wreckage of the Twin Towers didn't hang around on the sidewalk, pondering the impossibility of their task. They thrived on every rescue, remaining positive that they could get the job done. Whatever you're pushing your audience to do, be convinced of their inevitable victory.

BELIEVE IN YOURSELF

To motivate others, **U** have to believe in your skills as a motivator. You're not the weak link, but the anchor of the chain. No one likes being up there alone, open to criticism. We all fear saying something wrong, not conveying the right meaning, forgetting our lines. The fear of looking ridiculous stems from a lack of confidence. This lack is a self-fulfilling prophecy. If you don't believe you can do your job as a speaker, I 100% guarantee you'll mess up.

Improving self-confidence is something firefighters do all the time. They feel confident running into a burning structure because they learn to assess, attack, and survive. Firefighters know how fire reacts with different building materials, how it develops, and how to slow it down. They train, drill, and practice. Firefighters prepare. Preparation is as essential to speaking as it is to surviving an inferno. You have to know your material back to front, so that what you say is a bright, hopeful light to your audience. You're the chosen one. You've got the knowledge, and you know how to lay it down. The audience needs to hear what **U** have to say.

Practice your posture before you address your audience. Be alert. Put a little swagger in your step. Don't be stiff. Make eye contact. If you're speaking to a crowd, spread that eye contact around. Look confident and you'll feel confident. Everyone you're speaking to has special strengths, and so do you.

FOCUS ON YOUR AUDIENCE

Here's where empathy comes into play. If you pay attention to the looks and gestures of others, you can read their reaction to your message and adjust accordingly. Your goal here is to identify with your audience's emotions. For instance, if an audience member won't meet your eye, if he's tapping on the table, clicking a pen, doodling, etc., chances are he's bored. It's time to increase your tempo, maybe skip ahead to some engaging true-to-life illustration or funny anecdote.

If somebody's smiling, leaning back with their hands behind their head, and nodding along, it means you've got their full support. More than that, they feel confident about what you're saying. They feel good about the plans you're laying out. **U** can feed on their confidence to boost your own.

A person glaring at you or off into space, making sarcastic or cynical comments to their buddies, crossing their arms, or looking over their glasses is conveying disapproval. They're defensive, wanting to distance themselves from what's going on. It may be possible to pull them in by citing specific contributions they can make, using something they did right as a positive example. If this doesn't work, it's not your fault. Concentrate your energy on those with an open mind.

Frustration in an audience member shows up in lots of ways—pulling on ears, rubbing the face with a hand, aggressively scratching the head, making frequent changes in position. If several of your audience members are giving you these signals, it might be time to wrap up. If your audience is actively moving toward you, maintaining an open posture, they'll happily listen to you for several minutes more.

The secret to feeling out your audience is not to judge too quickly. Some of the behaviors listed above could be caused by environmental distractions or habits. The point is that whether you're speaking to one person or a thousand, communication is never give without take. You cue the audience, and the audience cues you. Using these suggestions as a guide will make it easier to connect with your audience, ensuring that they understand the true message you're working hard to convey.

. . . Breaks Down Defensive Attitudes

U won't always be preaching to the choir. City and corporate leaders may have different perspectives. Even those in your organization may be resistant to your attempts to connect. When I was working my first month as a fire prevention specialist, I was assigned to follow the lead of an experienced inspector. I'd heard stories about the guy. He was a Vietnam vet, a real hard case. Some people told me that he'd act borderline crazy every now and then. Since I'd been in the army, I felt I could communicate with nearly anyone. But I was about to learn that empathy demands more than knowing a person's background.

We began our day at the local hospital. As we passed through security on our way to meet our contact, the head of security recognized me and began a conversation. We spoke rapidly about family and current events. I felt good, having deepened a useful connection. As my fellow inspector and I worked our way down from the top floor, a department head came forward, asking how me and mine were doing, that sort of thing. I talked and listened politely to her story. But when I turned to join my group, I saw that they'd disappeared. It was like when David

Copperfield says, “Abracadabra!” I looked in every direction, but the group was gone. I called over personal radio. No answer. Eventually, I returned to security to wait. Three hours later, the older inspector and our escort arrived. At least I was well rested.

What I didn’t take into account in dealing with this situation was that the inspector expected me to know nothing, do nothing, talk to nobody. I didn’t have the time or rank to say boo to a goose. Demonstrating my ability to connect hit his insecurity button. He was quite sensitive, but in my experience, far from unique. I’ve encountered plenty of longtimers, in the fire service and elsewhere, who expect every rookie to be like a fly on the wall, without the buzzing. The inspector’s situation was sad, in retrospect. If he’d opened his mind and been ready to connect with some of the folks who were reaching out, his professional life could have been easier and more productive. His personal life might have benefited, too.

Many people are insecure in their positions and abilities. Some try to mask that insecurity by looking busy. If I stack a bunch of papers on my desk, people are going to assume I’m working hard. But if all those papers ever do is get shuffled around, somebody will eventually see through the ruse. Even efficient, productive people often worry that they’re not doing enough to stay off management’s radar. The whole basis of that fear is wrongheaded. If I’m doing a good job and the bosses can’t see it, I’m better off putting my energy into building peer influence.

A lot of people train themselves as kids to work just hard enough to get by, without drawing attention to themselves. A better approach is to use empathy to know where a defensive audience is coming from. By "defensive audience" I mean any person or group who resists your attempts to communicate. To connect with people like that, you need insight. Step back and ask yourself what the audience wants and why they're resistant. Do they feel threatened by your ideas? Maybe talking more about the benefit to them personally will help. Is there some personal tension between you and the audience, or a traditional distrust between a group you represent and them? Maybe you can win them over by emphasizing your need for their help.

Whatever your read on the audience, it's essential that **U** make a plan of action and carry it out. Here are some pointers:

- Remember that leadership is influence. Don't try to throw your weight around. Find mutual goals that will help you connect.
- Take your time. Influence is built slowly. As people see you're trustworthy, they'll come back to you with a more open attitude.
- Be willing to listen to problems and solutions. Don't take offense if somebody offers a suggestion that is different from yours. Rather than insisting on your own way, help the group make better decisions.
- Communicate each step of every plan. Surprises erode trust.
- Be honest about your motives. If you're promoting an idea, be open about talking about your inspiration. An observation that sparked you may win somebody over.
- Be proactive. Offer to educate members of your audience, as well as new recruits, prior to initiating any new action.

- Don't let your own ego, pride, title, or rank stand in the way of having an open mind.
- Be concerned for others. Where appropriate, explain how the ideas you're promoting will benefit your audience's friends and families, their prosperity, and well-being.
- Especially if your defensive audience is made up of fellow firefighters or others where teamwork is a matter of life and death, reaffirm your commitment to being there for them in time of need.

As you prepare yourself to communicate and connect, be aware that you will meet people who are downright hostile to your efforts. If **U** can offer them an advantage in some field of operation they care about, sometimes they'll perk up their ears. You'll be able to walk away from the confrontation with a new ally instead of an enemy. To be a leader, you need to connect with people who want to follow. Not everybody will immediately recognize that what you have to say is in their best interests. Be patient and follow the pointers above to increase your chances of success.

. . . Speaks to Minds and Hearts

People visiting Japan for the first time are often struck by the importance the Japanese place on exchanging business cards. An entire social ceremony has grown up around the act. Elegantly dressed folks sit on their knees, sipping tea and examining in minute detail the card stock, lettering, and design of cards provided by their fellow guests, before these are carefully tucked away. Why do the Japanese, who are among the most tech-savvy people in the world, place so much emphasis on this seemingly old-fashioned practice? Because the trendsetters in their business culture appreciate the importance of connecting.

When, in my early days as a sergeant in the army, I tried to lead by leaning on the authority of my position, I didn't get far. While you can certainly order soldiers to do nearly anything and eventually it will get done, there's a heap of difference between doing a job and doing it right. People will rise to the occasion in an emergency, but what about the essential nonemergency work, the day-to-day maintenance tasks, the preparation? That work can be equally important yet easy to neglect if those tasked with it are not motivated by trust and friendship with those who lead.

"The colossal misunderstanding of our time," wrote Rabbi Edwin H. Friedman, "is the assumption that insight will work with people who are unmotivated to change."

John C. Maxwell put it more simply: "People may hear your words, but they feel your attitude."

Your attitude can overtake the words you say, in both positive and negative ways. To communicate effectively, you must have passion, energy, and intensity. An elegant speaker who is lacking in these qualities may be quoted, but they will never be followed. Many of the most influential leaders in history were plainspoken, yet their words were empowered by the force of conviction. Nor are many words required. This is especially true in America. Abraham Lincoln's famous Gettysburg Address is a lean 272 words long, yet it inspired a nation on the verge of collapse to stand together.

Passion is a conviction that gets you personally fired up. **Energy** is the outward demonstration of that fire. **Intensity** reflects a deep sense of urgency felt by a speaker. We can boil these and several related concepts into a single trait: ***charisma***. Charisma makes an individual stand out in a crowd. People won't always remember everything a charismatic leader said, but they will remember how that leader made them feel.

How do **U** build charisma? Start by having a positive attitude. Have you noticed that people with positive attitudes pay more attention to others? They seem genuinely moved to listen and express appreciation for others' contributions and opinions. Thus, positivity is the most essential ingredient in the recipe for charisma. In the same way a pancake is more than flour, though, a positive attitude improves when you sweeten it up. What ingredients can we add to our charisma recipe?

Belief in yourself is essential. If you don't consider yourself trustworthy, no one else will either. You have to trust your insight, your judgment, and the rightness of what you're setting out to do. Positional leaders sometimes get the notion that since they're in charge, anything they say is as good as truth. To connect with those you lead, you have to communicate what you really believe to be true, having deeply examined it in your heart. Facts speak to the brain. An honest expression of your beliefs about those facts will speak to the heart.

Then add a focus on others. When you focus on what other people need, you can connect with them emotionally. "Need" is a feeling, after all. It can be negative, like when you feel a need for something you don't have. But it can also be positive, when someone steps forward to help meet that need. Offer to be the sort of person people can rely on. They'll be drawn to **U**.

Flashpoint Review!

- Whether speaking to an audience of one or many, believe in what you have to say, and take your time reading those who listen.
- Resistance to your ideas is no reason to give up. Be patient, empathize, and you can break through defenses.
- Give to your audience. Receive their response. Change your approach to match their energy.

Chapter Four: Communicate to Connect

Leaders have character. Leaders communicate. Keeping these truths in mind will help prepare **U** to get ahead in your chosen career. But if all you have is head knowledge, you won't advance. To thrive as a leader, you have to put knowledge into action. What's great about understanding leadership, character, and communication is that once you do, you're free to grow. You can't be limited by circumstances. A leader of strong character won't be limited by a lack of position. A leader who communicates won't be limited by a lack of seniority. A leader who connects won't need to wait for a promotion before stepping up as an influencer. By exercising character, communication skills, and the capability to connect, you free yourself from whatever forces are holding **U** back.

How does a VIP bring together character and communication skills to influence and lead? In this, our final chapter, we'll pull together everything we've talked about so far to show how you can communicate to connect Simply and Effectively. You'll see how you can grow your influence By Helping Others Connect and Grow. Finally, we'll discuss how cultivating the Essential Traits of a VIP will enable you To Safeguard Your Organization's Future.

. . . Simply and Effectively

Getting your point across to an individual is a matter of finding common goals and using empathy to get around defensiveness, as discussed in the previous chapter. Communicating to a group requires extra effort, because the more people you're talking to, the more simple you need to make your message. Instead of doing a data dump, giving your audience more information than they can consume, be specific and clear. Careful preparation is definitely worth it.

We've all seen speakers on TV talking to an audience while reading off a teleprompter. Making speech sound natural when you're being cued word for word is a challenge even for serious actors. Instead of trying to read a monologue, consider making short notes in an outline format. This opens **U** up to showing respect, genuineness, and empathy by responding to your audience's mood. Don't be afraid to skip a line here and there if folks are falling asleep and the good stuff is lower down. The less detail you put in your notes, the freer you'll feel to adapt. Just be sure to strike a balance, including enough detail that you won't forget to hit the main points.

Once your outline is in hand, ask for someone to give you feedback. Deliver your speech to one person, imagining that you're in front of your target audience. Note your helper's reaction during and after. Were the main points clear? Did your enthusiasm come across? Were your arguments persuasive? Receive the feedback without comment.

It's no fair attacking somebody for their opinion, especially if you drafted them to tell you the hard truth. In addition to getting someone to watch you, consider practicing in front of a camera. Habits you may not even be aware of leap out when you see them on video.

When **U** get in front of your audience, take a moment to acknowledge the efforts those in attendance took to be there. Try to set everybody at ease. You want the group to feel like you're all in a life raft together, taking turns whacking sharks with the oar. Making the audience feel at ease is especially important if you're about to discuss a difficult topic. Play off the energy of the crowd. I learned this from playing music. There's a vibe from my voice and my guitar, and another that flows back at me through looks, smiles, and folks feeling the beat. If I try to go against the crowd's rhythm, they'll get frustrated, often without even knowing the reason why. But if I get rowdy when they get rowdy, slow down when they're tired, etc., they will tip more, drink more, and have a better time.

Every speech has an introduction, a body, and a conclusion. In the intro, lay out what you want to accomplish. In the body, make an argument for doing things your way. In the conclusion, remind people of your main points, then present a "call to action." Hulk Hogan used to do this in the '80s, telling kids to "Train, say your prayers, and take your vitamins." He'd challenge opponents, "What'cha gonna do?" That's the essence of what you need to ask. Now that the audience is educated on the subject you've presented, what are they going to do in response? You're not asking for them to guess. If you've made your points clearly and strongly, they'll know the answer.

Following the conclusion, the job of leading by influence is not done. Ask people in the audience to share what they've learned. If you're conducting a training session or seminar, this would generally be done as part of your speech. If you're trying to persuade city leaders in a meeting, you might wait until after, seeking out those with whom you have a connection. Absorb the feedback you get in this way both for your own benefit and to reassure the other person that you're interested in his or her concerns. **U** weren't just talking to hear yourself. **U** want action.

After you've covered the material and made sure the audience heard, ask how your listeners are going to pass on what you've said. Help those who've taken the time to listen get excited about the task ahead. Taking on a daunting challenge can be intimidating or exhilarating. The difference is how prepared a person feels to do what needs to be done. We'll talk more about this in our next section.

To be effective, ask yourself:

- What am I asking my audience to do?
- What are the main points I need to communicate?
- How can I make those few points memorable?

That last question is worth pondering. No audience has an infinite attention span. To help them learn, you have to be clear and concise. Professor and Promise Keeper Howard Hendricks wrote that all communication is made up of three components, namely the intellectual, emotional, and volitional. When we communicate with others, we have to spend time on the thought, emotion, and action we're trying to inspire. *Thought* is the information we're relaying. *Emotion* conveys our feelings about what we say. *Action* is what we do with what we teach, the behaviors we'd like to see initiated.

If you go too far into the weeds, complicating what you say, some aspect of communication—thought, emotion, or action—is going to get lost. Next time you're tasked with conveying something, imagine you're standing in front of a group of elementary kids. Try to bring your topic down to their level. To make your *thought* clear, don't weigh it down with technical terms. Put *emotion* into your presentation so the importance of what you're saying doesn't go over the audience's head. When **U** call for *action*, make sure that action is appropriate to the audience. For example, if I were teaching a class of fourth graders about fire response, would it make sense for me to spend time on the differences between fighting a grease fire and an electrical fire? Of course not. What the kids need to know is how to get safely out of a bad situation and alert an adult. I'd instruct them on having a plan and detecting the signs of a blaze, then drill "stop, drop, and roll."

You can apply this same kind of thinking to speaking before an adult audience. Convey information, not jargon. Speak with passion, touching hearts. Connect with the audience on their level, being ready to follow through. If you do, you'll be empowered to get your point across, inspiring action in those who listen.

. . . By Helping Others Connect and Grow

Positional leaders, those who are placed in their leadership role by persons above, have the opportunity to use that role to expand influence.

The problem is that many don't see why they should bother. They equate rank with leadership, though these are really not the same. Rank and title are appointments that may or may not reflect individual merit. In an organization like the fire service, ranks are essential parts of the organizational structure. Those who hold rank and title are to be respected, for the sake of the job we all do. True leaders, though, are persons of influence. Rank and title are secondary considerations when it comes to evaluating the vital role they play.

As a representative for Police and Firemen's Insurance Association, I travel around to different departments. Being aware of leadership as I am, I can't help but became aware of the influential people within these organizations. One leader who comes to mind is Lieutenant John Russell from Huber Heights Fire Department in Dayton, Ohio. John is a training officer. He knows firefighting like the back of his hand. A master communicator, he's constantly connecting with students and members of the community. Everyone knows that if John says it, it's true. He teaches by doing and is known for having high morals and integrity. When I think of John, I don't picture his lieutenant insignia. I picture the brilliant smile of a VIP.

To an influence leader, rank is a tool. Connections, too, are tools in the hand of an influence leader. The difference is that a connector can lead by influence even without rank, but a high-ranking positional leader who doesn't connect can't use influence effectively. It's important to remember that surviving a crisis (life-threatening or otherwise) is not a solo act. None of us is Superman. To be effective, we have to work together. It should come as no surprise that to be an effective leader, the most vital skill **U** can learn is how to pass your knowledge on.

When you are communicating, teaching others to lead is your responsibility as a leader. With the right mindset, you can influence others to think positively, act positively, and get positive results. Start by getting to know the people you lead. Consider the following statements. How many are true about people in your circle of influence?

- I see this person's potential.
- I have a vision for their future.
- I know what their passion really is.
- I acknowledge their character flaws but see how addressing these will build a strong foundation.
- I am focused on their strengths. I don't advertise their weaknesses.
- If you can give affirmative responses about someone you're in a position to mentor, both you and that person are primed to excel. To help them reach the next level in their leadership, follow these guidelines:
- Take one step at a time.
- Put the right resources in their hands.
- Show them the big picture.
- Teach them to connect.
- The following are some tools to bring with you, and to pass on:
- A positive attitude
- The ability to relate and accept others
- Appreciation for personal and professional skills that advance the team

- The drive to educate up-and-coming leaders

By tailoring your message to an individual's personality, experience, and intellect, you open the door to them accepting what you say. The advice you give, based on your own experience, will help them grow into a leadership role. Like all the skills discussed in this book, you won't always get the best results on the first try. Keep looking for ways to help others take a step up. Keep your message simple. **U** will improve over time.

. . . To Safeguard Your Organization's Future

Learning to connect takes time. Organizationally, connecting requires higher-ups to value their future enough to invest in workshops and specialized training for new recruits. Being strapped for time and/or cash is no excuse. The danger of not setting energetic individuals on the path to building professional relationships is too great. Skilled leaders get voted out, seek advancement in other spheres, and retire. For the organization to survive, new blood must replace the old. What happens to an organization that has failed to train for the future? They wind up on the junk heap of history.

Without question, the go-getting twenty-something has a better chance of being around for the long haul than the sixty-something longtimer looking wistfully at the golf course across the street from his window. Provided, that is, that the department can give the twenty-something incentive to stay. It takes years to build the relationships needed for the new guard to successfully transition into positions of authority. Thankfully, new recruits to the organization have years to give. Some may have the background and disposition to learn how to connect on their own. Most will not.

It's safe to say that few twenty-somethings have learned the value of connecting. They may have thousands of "followers" on social media, but what influence does such a person actually have with these button-clickers? Leading means more than getting somebody to sign up for notifications about your latest status changes.

The best thing an organization can do to ensure its future is to connect aspiring VIPs with leaders who can pass on their skills. Then, get those educated young folks front and center. Test them under controlled conditions and let them learn from experience. To help a young person expand their influence and ambition, follow this three-step process:

Step 1: Assess the current environment. What programs exists to train aspiring leaders? If these do not exist inside your organization, look outside. Push for sponsorship in accredited programs. Ensure ambitious climbers are aware of their opportunities.

Step 2: Train VIPs to connect. This is where the time investment kicks in. Mentors in the organization must be willing to take experienced personnel under their wings, then give their students opportunities to shine. Has somebody in your organization been asked to speak at an event? Consider offering the assignment to an up-and-comer, with coaching from seasoned vets. "Learn by doing" is good advice, provided your trapeze act comes with a safety net.

Step 3: Build long-term relationships with a view to the future. Having taken the long view inside the organization, it's time to turn your perspective outward. Who in the community is demonstrating leadership qualities? As I've learned from personal experience, it's not always possible to tell. That's why it's important to cast a wide net, scooping up connections in every way you can. Try to look beyond a person's present circumstances to see the leader they can become. I'm speaking here about future community leaders, and the future movers-and-shakers in your industry, who are at the same level as your young climbers are now. Consider the influence individuals outside your organization may come to have in the fullness of time. Get your blossoming VIPs in the same room.

Having friends in high places doesn't just happen. It takes time and preparation. If you're reading this guide, no doubt you have an interest in seeing your organization prosper, even as your efforts at self-improvement benefit your career. If you're a young, rising leader, look for opportunities now to build influence both inside and outside the chain of command. If you are a seasoned professional with some years under your belt, reach out to those newbies who are going to make or break the organization in years to come. It's never too early or too late to learn to communicate. As **U** reach out to others, your influence will increase. You'll find new ways to communicate, connect, and build your future.

Flashpoint Review!

- Convey your theme in as few points as possible. Tell the audience what you want them to think, feel, and do.
- Look for ways to pass on what you know, developing future leaders.
- There are always opportunities to connect in your community. Once you know how, nothing can hold you back.

About the Author

From 2016 to the present, Brian Benedict has served as the Midwest regional sales manager for Police and Firemen's Insurance Association, managing up to sixty representatives in departments from Ohio to Colorado. He has trained both new and veteran department representatives, imparting insurance product information and innovating sales and service techniques, all while also performing interviewing and hiring duties. Personal experience making presentations to multiple fire departments has taught him much about how to connect.

During the twenty-year period from 1996 to 2016, Brian held active employment as a firefighter, gaining the following training and certifications:

- Firefighter 1 & 2
- Engineer (Driver Operator)
- EMT—Emergency Medical Technician
- Hazardous Materials—B
- Technical Rescue Awareness
- Fire Officer 1 & 2
- Fire Instructor
- Fire Inspector 1 & 2

- Fire Investigator
- CFEI—Certified Fire & Explosion Investigator
- Homeland Security Bomb School, New Mexico Tech
- ATF Post Blast Investigative Techniques
- Various Fire Investigation classes through Indiana Public Safety Institute
- Arson Investigator—National Fire Academy, Maryland
- Courtroom Testimony Course for Arson Investigators

He held positions as a firefighter, heavy rescue driver operator, lieutenant, inspector, investigator, and fire prevention specialist, teaching classes to elementary, junior high, and high school students, as well as local businesses. As needed, he filled in as battalion chief. Other positions include fire marshal (deputy chief of fire prevention), member of Indiana Fire Inspectors Association, and member of International Arson Association.

Brian's involvement with Police and Firemen's Insurance Association dates from 2008. In that year, he began work as a department representative for East Indiana and Western Ohio. He is proud of the work he has done and continues to do, serving police and firefighters with insurance products and fraternal protection.

Prior to entering the fire service, Brian worked for Cellular One in Dayton, Ohio. Between 1991 and 1996, he held positions as a technician, account executive, and customer service supervisor. He credits Cellular One with giving him his early training as a connector. Thanks to their programs, he learned the importance of interpersonal relationships, networking, communication, and putting service first. To this day, he strives for the win-win.

To know where somebody's coming from, you have to know where they've been. The legacy of military service that included grandfathers Daniel Woodman and Fortis Benedict, US Army, and father Phillip Benedict, US Air Force, had a powerful influence on Brian and his twin brother Bruce. Brian served five years as a wire systems installer in the army, advancing to the rank of sergeant. He carried out duty assignments in Fort Jackson, SC; Fort Gordon, GA; Fort Bragg, NC; and Karlsruhe, Baden-Württemberg, Germany. He completed the US Army Non-Commissioned Officer Academy and Primary Leadership Development Course. Bruce Benedict retired as a US Army Major, having worked in intelligence, with three tours in Iraq and Afghanistan and many assignments throughout the world. He still consults with intelligence professionals in Quantico, VA, and Washington, DC.

In addition to this lifetime of learning, Brian would like to acknowledge the transformative effect the John Maxwell Leadership Team has had on his outlook. As a team member since 2016, Brian is certified as a John Maxwell Leadership Speaker, Trainer, and Coach.

Last but by no means least, he wishes to thank his loving wife, Lisa Benedict, for nineteen years of patience and support. Having worked as a practice manager at GYN Reid Hospital, Lisa recently received her MBA in health care management. She currently works as an instructor at IVY Tech College. Raising daughter Jessi and sons Skyler and Dylan has been a team effort, and a rewarding one.

You can catch up with Brian, connect on Facebook and Twitter, and schedule workshops to Build the Business of "U" at www.BrianBenedict.com.

CPSIA information can be obtained
at www.ICGtesting.com
Printed in the USA
LVOW05s0624141217
559682LV00024B/1427/P

9 781979 032131